GARIBALDI

Garibaldi

GARIBALDI

The Legend and the Man

By

PETER de POLNAY

GREENWOOD PRESS, PUBLISHERS
WESTPORT, CONNECTICUT

Library of Congress Cataloging in Publication Data

De Polnay, Peter, 1906-
   Garibaldi : the legend and the man.

   Reprint of the ed. published by Hollis & Carter,
London.
   Bibliography: p.
   Includes index.
   1. Garibaldi, Giuseppe, 1807-1882.
DG552.8.G2D4 1976   945'.08'0924 [B]   75-22641
ISBN 0-8371-8361-8

Originally published in 1960 by Hollis & Carter, London

Reprinted with the permission of Peter de Polnay

Reprinted in 1976 by Greenwood Press,
a division of Williamhouse-Regency Inc.

Library of Congress Catalog Card Number 75-22641

ISBN 0-8371-8361-8

Printed in the United States of America

CONTENTS

ILLUSTRATIONS

I

FROM NICE TO ROME

I

GIUSEPPE GARIBALDI was born in Nice on 4th July 1807, the son of Domenico Garibaldi and Rosa Raimondi. He saw light in a small house in the Quai Lunel, which has since changed its name to Quai Cassini. Nice, at the time, belonged to France; thus he was born a subject of the Emperor Napoleon I.

In a letter he wrote to his wife, Anita, Garibaldi observed: "Happy my mother to have brought me into the world at such a beautiful epoch for Italy." Happy Garibaldi, too, for he was made for his time: he could not have created it. He could never bring about the right moment, but if the right moment came Garibaldi invariably appeared with uncanny swiftness and mastered it admirably. Twice he tried to create the moment: at Aspromonte in 1862 and Mentana in 1867. In each case he failed miserably.

During his lifetime many biographies were written about him, some of which were quite fantastic. He did not give them the lie. It was as if a man walked past his statues and pretended not to notice that he was taller and more imposing in stone and marble than in the looking-glass. It is true that Garibaldi said in his *Memorie* published in 1872 that, for instance, Alexandre Dumas's (Père) *Autobiography of Garibaldi* was somewhat romantic if not unreliable, but otherwise Garibaldi was not the man to try to harm his own legend, in which he believed as profoundly as those who came under its influence, which does not mean that some of them did not influence him more than was good for him.

The legend has it that he was born at sea in a thunderstorm. For a man who would be hailed as an almost supernatural figure a thunderstorm at sea was certainly a fitting beginning. The small house where little Giuseppe and his parents lived stood beside the sea. The father was a fisherman, the mother the son worshipped, but both father and mother, so Theodore Bent, another contemporary biographer, points out, were, alas, priest-trodden, though, Bent had to admit, they were a happy, devoted couple.

The boy was not given to studying, did not play games, went for long walks in the mountains, in short was different from other boys. He was taught by a M. Arena, a friend of his father, and one day M. Arena met the small boy sitting with a book in his lap, gazing out to sea.

"What are you doing?" asked M. Arena.

"I am reading," answered the boy.

"But you are not looking at your book."

"That's true."

"Then what were you reading?"

"I was reading the sky and the sea."

"And what do they tell you?"

"I don't know," said the boy candidly, "but it seems to me that I read there finer things than I could find in books made of paper."

Camille Leynadier, who reproduced in his *Mémoires Authentiques sur Garibaldi* that dialogue, might have recorded the truth. Garibaldi could have spoken like that.

In his childhood, according to Alexandre Dumas, the only physical exercise he indulged in was swimming, which seems to contradict the ramblings in the mountains. As a swimmer he saved several lives. Legend has it that at the age of eight he saved the life of a drowning washer-woman. He must have been a powerful swimmer, or perhaps the washerwoman was an extraordinarily light washerwoman.

The father was said to be a merchant skipper too, and blued whatever money came his way. Yet his son gratefully acknowledged that of all the money he scattered to the winds that which he spent on his son's education gave him the greatest pleasure. Garibaldi went on to say through his mouthpiece Dumas, his education was by no means of the superior kind. His father did not have him taught either gymnastics, or the use of arms, or horsemanship. He learnt gymnastics by climbing into the shrouds on ships and letting himself glide along the ropes. Fencing he learnt when defending his own head and when doing his best to split those of others, horsemanship from the gauchos in South America. Beside M. Arena a Father Giovanni was his teacher too, and he remembered Father Giovanni gratefully in spite of his having been a priest.

Garibaldi went to sea at the age of thirteen, first with his father, then in the brigantine *Etna*. Later on he made several voyages to the Eastern Mediterranean and the Black Sea. Before that he had, however, his first love affair with a Majorcan girl called Beppa. She and Garibaldi were of the same age, saw each other daily; her father was a fisherman. The girl's and the boy's love was revealed through the sacred flame of patriotism. Beppa's father was a political exile, who had to flee Spain in 1815. One day when the father, the boy and the girl were together, the boy asked the girl's father what love of one's country meant. The question was eloquently answered by the father, in fact he initiated Garibaldi into the mystery of the resurrection of nations. Deeply moved, Garibaldi fell in love with Beppa.

Another day Beppa and her father went out in their small boat to get mussels off the rocks. The sea was calm, the sun shone, in short nothing could make one suspect that a violent storm was brewing. When it burst, Beppa and her father tried to row back to the jetty. The waves threw the frail boat against the jetty, smashing her. It had become dark, and in the darkness rose a sonorous voice, the voice of Garibaldi, whose fear for the loved one had driven him to the jetty. Beppa and her father held on to what was left of the smashed boat. He could hardly distinguish anything in the blackness.

"Save my father," cried the heroic girl.

"Save my daughter," shouted the brave father.

The long and the short of it was that the powerful swimmer succeeded in saving the father. The daughter perished. With a broken heart Garibaldi took to seafaring. By then Nice had been restored to the Sardinian king. (That was in 1815. Though no date is given for the above episode, one feels that even a person of Garibaldi's capacities was surely more than eight years old at the time.)

In the course of one of his sea voyages on board the *Clorinda*, he met a party of Saint-Simonians who were going to Constantinople. He fell under their spell, that is he became imbued with Claude de Rouvroy Saint-Simon's teachings, which, one might say, were the start of his journey towards final atheism. The Saint-Simonian doctrines were, almost *par excellence*, right for the sentiments and imagination of a young uneducated mind. Though Saint-Simon was practically the founder of French socialism, he and his disciples considered his book *New Christianity* as a new religion. His doctrines insisted on the claims of merit, as long as merit had nothing to do with the feudal and military systems. (Saint-Simon was born in 1760 in Paris and died in 1825.) He wanted industrial leaders to control society, the basis being "each man according to his merit," which meant his capacity for work. His Social Individual is man and woman, associated in the exercise of the triple functions of religion, the state and family. George Jacob Holyoake, the Rationalist, tells us that it was the custom of Saint-Simonians, when they thought that the appropriate moment had come, to spread the rumour of their deaths, then vanish. Saint-Simon himself attempted suicide two years before his death.

Young Garibaldi found the Saint-Simonians exhilarating. Their religion was so different and so new compared to Father Giovanni's and M. Arena's teachings, especially as the apostles of the new creed assured him that a man who, by becoming cosmopolitan, adopts some other country as his own and makes offer of his sword and his blood to every people struggling against tyranny, is more than a soldier: he is a hero. "Strange glimmerings," Garibaldi relates through Dumas, "now began to illuminate my mind, by the aid of which I saw a ship, no longer as a vehicle charged with the mission of exchanging the goods of one country for those of another, but as a winged messenger bearing the word of the Lord and the sword of the Archangel." Dumas certainly put it on thick.

And here it should be explained what Dumas had to do with Garibaldi's childhood and youth. As a matter of fact he had nothing to do with them. What happened was this: Dumas came to Italy in 1860 in search of what is known today as copy. Nobody could have been better copy during the Risorgimento than General Garibaldi. Dumas arrived in Turin, the capital of Piedmont, and H. A. d'Ideville, the French diplomat and diarist who had met him once before in Eugéne Delacroix's studio in Paris, wished to take his fellow countryman to the Marchesa Alfieri, Count Cavour's niece. Dumas refused.

"Do you want to know why?" he asked M. d'Ideville. "I will tell you. I might meet her uncle Count Cavour. I want that under no circumstances whatever. This is the reason: I am leaving Turin in twenty-four hours, I will embark in Genoa and in three days' time I shall be with Garibaldi [in Sicily]. I have not met him yet but have written to him, he is waiting for me. That man is a hero, a sublime adventurer, a character for a novel. With him, through him I want to achieve something. C'est un fou, c'est un niais . . . mais un niais heroïque. . . . What could I do with Cavour? Cavour is a great statesman, a consummate politician, a man of genius. He is bigger than Garibaldi—as if I did not know. But he does not wear a red shirt! . . . I am an artist and Garibaldi alone attracts me."

The author of *Monte Cristo* went duly to meet Garibaldi, and the two flamboyant personages fell enraptured into each other's arms, much to the annoyance of another less flamboyant but equally insistent biographer, namely Mme Schwartz, alias Elpis Melena. Garibaldi recompensed Dumas for his scoop by appointing him Superintendent of Arts in Naples after he entered the capital of the Two Sicilies. "Dumas," M. d'Ideville observed laconically, "spent the Neapolitan gold with his customary generosity."

So Alexandre Dumas recorded Garibaldi's youth, and some of the South American adventures Garibaldi did not include in his *Memorie*. In Dumas's version Garibaldi's first visit to Rome as a sailor is briefly recorded in a flowery passage; when Garibaldi via Dumas recalls the visit the impressions are already those of the rabid anticlerical into whom he had not yet developed at the time of his visit.

The visit to Rome is more picturesque in Leynadier's version, and since it was read at the time and helped in

forming the image, it is worth repeating. Besides, it is as
romantic as the age required.

 One night while in Rome Garibaldi, sad and weighed
down by thought, walked about in the Coliseum, which
the moon lit up from end to end, and suddenly he heard
a voice singing in melancholic tones:

> Giuriam'! giuriam'! di sporgere
> Il sangue dei tiranni!
> Giuriam'! che avranno i figli
> La dolce Libertà!

The voice and the song in the middle of the night and
among the august ruins were the answer to the sombre
patriotic thoughts that obsessed Garibaldi. He went towards the singer, who, however, vanished before he
reached him. On the spot where the singer had stood, the
full moon picked out a name engraved on a stone. It was
the name of Ciro Menotti. Garibaldi doffed his hat
respectfully, bowed his head and surrendered his heart to
the memory of the great martyr of Italy.

 Among the many martyrs of Italy, who were mostly
caught through incompetence and consequently made into
martyrs, Ciro Menotti was outstanding. When the July
Revolution broke out in Paris the Italian liberals believed
that their hour had struck. Ciro Menotti was a subject
of Francis IV of Modena, and the duke was first well
disposed towards Menotti and his fellow liberals, that is
towards the Carbonari revolutionaries, but when Vienna
heard of the duke's attitude, the duke speedily changed it.
Menotti found out and denounced the duke's duplicity in
a letter he wrote on 7th January 1831 to Enrico Misley.
Nevertheless, he continued to conspire as if he were
unaware of the duke's double-dealing. Menotti went to
Florence in the course of January to solicit help from two

fellow Carbonari, Charles-Napoleon and Louis-Napoleon
Bonaparte. They did not come to Modena. Menotti
returned and fixed the date of the rising for the 3rd
February. All that under the duke's nose.

With fifty-eight conspirators he waited on that date in a
house for his rebel forces to arrive and start the rising.
Instead of the rebels the police and the ducal militia
appeared. Menotti and his comrades decided not to
surrender, so the house was besieged, even pieces of
artillery were brought up. The siege lasted for two hours,
at the end of which Menotti and his companions had no
ammunition left. They had hoped that the other rebels for
whom they had been waiting would come to their rescue.
Help did not materialize. Menotti had suddenly the queer
notion that he would go to the duke and speak to him as
man to man; a queer notion indeed, since they had risen
against him, and he of all people was perfectly acquainted
with the duke's attitude, of which the presence of police,
militia and cannons was proof enough. He jumped out
through a back window of the beleaguered house, drop-
ping into a side street, and was immediately hit in the
shoulder by a bullet, then captured. On 26th May Menotti
was shot.

It was the same Duke of Modena who ten years previously had instituted judicial proceedings against another
group of conspirators. Of the three hundred and fifty
persons arrested, fifty-six were condemned to death,
though only a few of them were executed. The rest were
imprisoned, but many of them escaped, including Antonio
Panizzi, who was to become the Librarian of the British
Museum, and one of the best propagandists of Italia Unita
in England. What, one wonders, could Menotti have
expected from Francis IV of Modena, even if he had
succeeded in seeing him on the fateful night?

To return to Garibaldi in the moonlight in the Coliseum. Standing beside Menotti's name he bitterly addressed Rome, the town of the Caesars and the Popes. Rome of the Caesars had been the bestial town of gladiators from Germany, Gaul and Thrace, of lions from Africa, and courtesans from Spain. "A dying gladiator," he said to Rome and the night, "fights against agony. Quick! pierce him with your staff. Perhaps he has a few drops of blood left. You can see it run. Drink it, savage beast! Leave the rest to the hyenas!" About the Rome of the Popes he was just as uncomplimentary. "And you, Rome of the Popes, arena of traffickers . . . bastard, degenerate sons of Christ. . . ."

"Enough, young man," cried the voice of the returned singer pointing at the name of Menotti. Garibaldi grasped his hand in silence. Thus two noble hearts came to understand each other. The other noble heart turned out to be nobody else than Angelo Brunetti, known as Ciceruacchio, who was to become the leader of the Trasteverin mob in the days of the Roman Republic, which his son helped to bring about by stabbing to death Count Pellegrino Rossi, the Pope's minister.

II

Garibaldi was twenty-one years old and second in command of the brig *Cortese* when he met an Englishman for the first time. Three times the *Cortese* was attacked by pirates during her voyage to the Black Sea, the first occasion being at Cape Matapan, and they were left with practically nothing by the plundering Greeks. When the brig arrived at St Nicolas an Englishman took pity on the barefooted young man in rags and gave him a pair of shoes. "When I look back on it now," Garibaldi wrote in 1870 in a letter to *Cassell's Magazine*, "I cannot help remembering that it was the first of many acts of kindness which bind me with such strong and lasting ties of gratitude to your noble nation."

They were captured twice more by pirates who took even the rags off the sailors' backs. The poor fellows had to cover themselves with matting, which the pirates overlooked. Again an Englishman, a Captain Taylor, came to their rescue, making it possible for them to proceed to Constantinople.

In spite of his close relations with England and enthusiastic English admirers and followers, and in spite of his long sojourn in the United States, in spite too of nearly marrying an Englishwoman, he did not become proficient in the language. His native tongue was the Nizard patois, and French and Italian became his two languages. Though he had had little education, he knew how to express himself forcefully in letters, and his unbridled pen could be fast indeed.

It was in 1834 that he first came into active contact with conspiracy. The head of the conspiracy was—one would almost say of course—Giuseppe Mazzini. Since Mazzini and Garibaldi were to cross one another's path throughout the Risorgimento, one feels here justified in drawing a picture of the man who was one of the four architects of Italian unity. The other three were King Victor Emmanuel II, Count Camillo Cavour and Garibaldi. There are few people thrown on each other by circumstances who had as little in common as Garibaldi and Mazzini.

Mazzini was the son of a well-to-do Genoese Dr Giacomo Mazzini, an earnest and stern man. His mother, Maria, was a woman of intellect; also a Jansenist. The son was born in 1805 in Genoa, and entered the university at the age of fifteen to study medicine. He who would in badly organized conspiracies send many fellow Italians to death, and who advocated the murder of despots, left the university because his highly sensitive nature could not withstand the ordeal of the operating table. He first joined the Carbonari, but in time considered it outmoded, and founded Young Italy.

Mazzini was an exceptionally handsome man. He had a fresh, clear complexion, shaded by long black hair, a noble forehead, a sweet though vivacious expression of steadfast resolution and inflexible determination, and these, together with the bright flashes of his dark eyes, combined to render him the most beautiful being, male or female, found Enrico Mayer, the Tuscan educator. With them went great intellectual power and disregard of vexing details.

After six months' imprisonment in the fortress of Savona in 1830 Mazzini took to the life of the exile. Marseilles was his first stop; in time London became his home. Though to ways and means he often attached insufficient importance Mazzini knew unhesitatingly what he wanted. He wanted a united Italy brought about by revolution, and without revolution there should be and could be no free Italy. For Garibaldi, who fought for it as a child might fight to put an end to the rule of grown-ups, liberty alone mattered, and by liberty he meant "Out with the stranger!" Garibaldi became an atheist and would declare that the Catholic Church should be extirpated throughout the world. He never bothered to think out how that could be achieved. But he was no thinker, and if one is allowed to transpose a French expression, then one could describe him as an atheist of the Café de Commerce.

However, Mazzini was very much a believer. He believed in his own convictions, which were God and the People. Christ would manifest Himself through the people, thus the people would become the People. Without belief in God, Mazzini said, no political enthusiasm could be created or sustained. Needless to say, such niceties had no appeal for Garibaldi, who was to remark that Mazzini was a man of theory, not of practice, who always spoke of the people, though he did not know who the people were. If the door was not properly locked on Garibaldi, so to speak, he would shoot out and try to make a dash for Rome; Mazzini believed in subversion, in bringing down the Church from within. He was a far more dangerous enemy.

God and the People; and when the Carlyles befriended him and he paid regular visits to them in Chelsea Mazzini expounded his doctrines to the Sage. God, said Mazzini, would reveal his New Word to "the People who in their collective intelligence would propound it".

"The people!" Carlyle exclaimed. "The ignorant, blind, vicious masses, chiels and fools to be regarded as teachers, leaders, guides? . . . No! . . . In verity they were to be taught, led, guided, if need be constrained to obey the superior wisdom and virtue of the chosen few!"

If Mazzini and Carlyle could have looked into this century they would have found a compromise when Mussolini and Hitler became the will incarnate of the People. And speaking of Mussolini, it is probable that he studied Garibaldi's methods of having and moving around a private army; but theory he learnt from the gentle, handsome Mazzini's teachings.

It was in conspiring and plotting that Mazzini expressed his practical self. Holyoake, who saw much of him in London, said that he detested cabinets and generals who employed spies. Nevertheless he made war by secrecy—open war being impossible to him—though never by treachery. Some who had suffered and were incensed by personal outrage or maddening oppression would act as spies in revenge. Mazzini was accused of inspiring them and employing them.

With his conspiracies and plots Mazzini succeeded in annoying Jane Carlyle, who rather loved him. In a letter to the Sage in August 1843 she wrote: "The Italian Revolution has begun and also, I suppose, ended". She found Mazzini in a state of violent excitement and she could not help telling him that "a Harrow or Eton schoolboy who uttered such nonsense would be whipped and expelled from the community as a mischievous blockhead". She went as far as to say she considered quite seriously whether it was not her duty as Mazzini's friend to warn the Austrian Government of the plans which he had confided in her "to save his head and those of the many at the sacrifice of the few".

Now Garibaldi the seafarer, the son of the fisherman, the natural leader of men on horseback to be, who was not given to secrecy and for whom the sword was mightier than the pen, came into the life of the plotter through a plot which was hatched by Mazzini and General Ramorino, who was called a drunkard, a gambler and a traitor after the failure of the plot. In the course of the Risorgimento the word traitor was much bandied about. Anyway, the unsuccessful Mazzinians were convinced that Ramorino sold them to the French, who then notified the Piedmontese authorities. Ramorino had had a fine record as a soldier while fighting in Poland.

Mazzini decided on the military occupation by his two columns coming from Switzerland of the village of San Giuliano, where they would link up with patriotic Savoyards and French Republicans, then the standard of the insurrection would be raised. Ramorino received forty thousand francs to defray the expenses of the expedition. He was in charge of one column, a Pole called Grabsky of the second. The Genevese, who wanted trouble neither with France nor Piedmont, did not care for those two columns assembling there, and when Ramorino's column reached the rendezvous they waited in vain for Grabsky's. Grabsky's column had set sail in two barques, but a Government steamer went in pursuit, seized the arms and arrested the men. Instead of continuing on the road to San Giuliano, Ramorino marched his men, Italians sprinkled with Polish volunteers, along the shores of the Lake of Geneva. Mazzini marched with them, and tried several times to find out from Ramorino what his plans were. He did not succeed in eliciting a satisfactory answer.

They halted for the night in Carra. Mazzini and Ramorino shared the same room. Mazzini had been feeling ill since the start of the expedition and was now running a high fever. He became suspicious. Where were they going? He urged the general, who had not taken off his cloak, to lead them where they could put their sacred cause to the test. "If victory be impossible, let us, at least, prove to Italy that we know how to die." Ramorino said he would regard it as a crime needlessly to expose his diminished troops to danger. Mazzini's answer was that there is no religion without its martyrs; they should establish theirs with their own blood.

His words were followed by firing. Mazzini took a rifle, and thanked God that he was brought at last face to face with the enemy—then the sick man collapsed. When he came round he was back in Switzerland. His comrades had carried him thither. Ramorino had ordered the retreat, and that was the end of the San Giuliano affair for Mazzini and his two columns. Some unfortunate French republicans, who entered Piedmont in the hope of joining up with the two columns, were attacked by Sardinian troops and dispersed after a fight. Two were made prisoners, and they were condemned to death and shot in Chambéry. Mazzini returned to his work.

Still it was that lamentable business which started Garibaldi on his true career; for he became involved for the first time. He enlisted, on the order of the conspirators, in the Sardinian Navy as a common sailor, and his task was to help to bring about a mutiny in the *Eurydice*, then seize the ship for the republican cause. When, however, Garibaldi heard of a proposed rising in Genoa he deserted and landed in that town. The idea was to capture the barracks of the gendarmes in the Piazza di Sarzana. On landing in Genoa from a boat he had stolen from the *Eurydice* he made immediately for the Piazza di Sarzana, where he waited for two hours for the other conspirators. At the end of the two hours troops appeared and surrounded the square, so Garibaldi left hurriedly. Logically he had no wish to return to the *Eurydice*, and made for his home-town Nice, dressed as an ordinary countryman, thanks to a woman into whose shop he had entered on the spur of the moment after the soldiers had come to the Piazza di Sarzana. It took him ten days to reach Nice. He did not want to frighten his mother, so went to stay with an aunt, remaining with her for a day. On the next day he swam the River Var. Now he was in France, he considered himself safe, but got arrested by the coastguards at the customs house. They explained they would keep him till instructions arrived from Paris, and took him first to Grasse, then to Draguignan, where he was locked in a room, the window of which was only fifteen feet from the ground. He jumped through the window and escaped.

On the following evening he reached an inn, and ordered food and wine. He ate and drank heartily, and the innkeeper congratulated him on his appetite. Garibaldi explained he had not eaten for some time, and after a while blurted out that he had escaped from Draguignan. The innkeeper told him that he felt it his duty to arrest him and hand him over to the authorities. Garibaldi laughed and suggested that the innkeeper should wait till he reached the dessert. The inn filled up, the proprietor continued to keep an eye on him, though he did not mention arrest again. Garibaldi jingled the few coins he had in his pocket, which seemed to put the innkeeper's mind at rest. Garibaldi sang "Le Dieu des Bonnes Gens" in his attractive tenor voice. The customers liked the song a lot, and asked him to sing more couplets, which he did, watching the innkeeper from the corner of his eye. His success was such that the innkeeper forgot about the arrest altogether, and the night was spent in drinking, singing and playing. The entire company accompanied him for six miles when he left at dawn. When he reached Marseilles he read in a newspaper that he had been condemned to death as a deserter from the Sardinian Navy. The newspaper was called *Le Peuple Souverain*. Soon after that he saved the life of a boy from drowning.

III

"Many of my friends," Garibaldi told Dumas, "had told me that above all I was a poet. If the test of being a poet is that one has written the *Iliad*, or the *Divine Comedy*, or the *Meditations of Lamartine*, or *Les Orientales* of Victor Hugo, then I am not a poet, but if spending hours in seeking in the deep blue waters of the sea the mysteries of submarine vegetation is being a poet; or if being entranced at the sight of the Bay of Rio de Janeiro, or of Naples, or of Constantinople makes one a poet; or if to meditate amid balls and bullets on filial tenderness and the memories of childhood or early love, without a thought that your dream may be rudely shattered by getting your head broken or having your arm carried away—then I am a poet."

Constantinople he had already visited several times, the Bay of Naples was still in the dim, glorious future: Rio de Janeiro followed, as it were, on the heels of Marseilles in 1836. He landed there from the brig *Nautonnier*, and was to stay in South America till 1848.

Garibaldi's lucky star could not have chosen a more suitable continent for the development of Garibaldi and the Garibaldi legend. South America was then and in many ways still is the continent of men. To be a man is essential, to be a man is the beginning and the end, and you have to prove on every occasion that you are one. You have to swagger as befits a man, draw your gun like a man, dress like a man, bang the table like a man, and take other men's women like a man, though at the same time protect your woman like a man. In short it is the continent of *cojones*, with which Garibaldi was well endowed. The South American period also gave his biographers all possible scope to exercise their imagination; and let it be added that Garibaldi did not lack imagination either.

"The *Memorie*," wrote Giuseppe Bandi, "are naturally the best means to reconstruct the South American life of Garibaldi, but they should not be taken for gospel truth. We do not want to insinuate that Garibaldi could lie or change facts; he was incapable of doing that. He was a writer rich in patriotism but often lacked historical or political sense, and could be forgetful of what might interest posterity."

In Rio de Janeiro he found many other Italian exiles, who helped him to buy a small vessel with which he could earn his living as a trader. An old friend from Genoa advanced some of the money, and found the rest by telling

others what a hero Garibaldi would have been in the cause
of Italy if he had been given the chance. The money was
collected, the ship was bought. Though he was never to
care for money, covet it or keep it, and in spite of never
taking advantage of the many opportunities that came
his way to enrich himself, he always found the people,
in fact the people found him, who would put even their
last penny at his disposal. Perhaps it was because he was
financially the least greedy of men. Many years later Pope
Pio Nono was to remark that only he and Garibaldi made
nothing out of the Risorgimento; and Pio Nono had no
cause to praise him.

Garibaldi made no money with trading. "Of myself I
can only say that as yet fortune does not smile upon my
endeavours," he wrote to a friend, and in a letter to his
brother he said: "Money, money is what we need most."

Tired of unsuccessful trading, Garibaldi entered the
service of the Republic of Rio Grande, which was at war
with the Emperor of Brazil. He became a privateer. His
first ship, the *Mazzini*, did not have a long life. Meeting a
Brazilian schooner, the *Mazzini* bore down on her, the
schooner surrendered, was boarded, and the *Mazzini*,
being no longer needed, was sunk: Garibaldi sailed for the
River Plate in the schooner. At Montevideo he sold some
of the coffee he found in the holds of the schooner to a
local merchant, who did not show any desire to pay him.
Garibaldi held him up at the point of his pistol, and the
merchant paid the two thousand patacoons he owed. On
the following morning he weighed anchor and sailed up
the River Plate. Garibaldi was off.

It is anybody's guess whether the fantastic fights and
battles that followed were exaggerated or not; whether
some of them could really have taken place; whether
Garibaldi romanced in retrospect; but it can be taken for

granted that whenever a fight or a battle came his way he was in the midst of it, which is, after all, what truly matters. There have been and will be varied opinions on Garibaldi. For the Garibaldians he was a shining hero who could do no wrong; for many others he was irresponsible and a charlatan; for Cavour, a pain in the neck; for Mazzini, often a fool; but whether one likes him or not, whether one considers him great or just Dumas's *niais*, his courage could never be doubted. As a warrior he was among the bravest, physical cowardice was simply unknown to him, and when one thinks of his actions or judges them, one has to bear in mind that rare quality: the complete absence of fear.

In one of his sea battles he got himself nearly killed by a bullet, lay half-conscious on deck and thought he was dying. He asked his friend Carniglia that if he died he should not be buried at sea, but on the sand, so that there should be an inscription on his tomb, some lines from Ugo Foscolo. The schooner put into the port of Gualeguay in the Argentine and Garibaldi was thrown into prison.

When he recovered from his wound he was allowed, on giving his word of honour not to escape, to go and live with a Spanish family. The authorities did not bother much about him, therefore he reached the conclusion that they were not interested in his word of honour either. So he escaped, but was recaptured. He was brought back to Gualeguay, where he was tortured. A contemporary writer related that even in old age Garibaldi could not speak of that ordeal without a shudder. He was suspended by his wrists for two hours outside the door of a shanty, yet he would not give away any of his accomplices. He remained in prison for two months, then they let him go without bringing him to trial.

He returned to Rio Grande and to buccaneering. He

was successful both on land and sea. The Brazilians feared
him, and his exploits were the talk of Latin America. In
time he became known as El Diablo.

In the course of one of his exploits, so *Les Mémoires
Authentiques* tell us, he and his followers found themselves
in the pampas of Uruguay. The pampas were covered with
grass eight to ten feet high, the only tracks were made by
buffaloes and bisons. (Tigers, according to Leynadier, were
also to be found in South America in those days.) Now
and then they flushed a bear or a bison. Garibaldi had an
Indian guide, who suddenly turned to him and cried:
"Ah kapa! Echeaa pah kaps!" That, apparently, meant
that there was trouble ahead. Right he was; for they soon
saw a prairie fire approaching. At the same moment
countless buffaloes, bisons, horses, deer, in short all the
varied inhabitants of the pampas, came thundering past.
Soon they were choking from smoke.

There was not a moment to be lost.

They followed the animals towards the south as fast as
they could, rightly convinced that the animals were
following their instincts. Unfortunately the fire was faster
than Garibaldi and his men. Garibaldi and the Indian
advanced in the smoke in front of the men, and after a
while found a buffalo track. "Throw away your powder
and follow me," said the Indian. Garibaldi obeyed, and
hurrying along the smouldering track they reached a
hillock and safety. They spent the night there in the middle
of the sea of fire; by the morning the danger was past. But
they were hungry. The Indian came to the rescue. With
a loud shout he pointed at an immense rattlesnake, and
being a Frenchman, Leynadier could not resist pointing out
that the serpent was perfectly grilled. With their knives
they cut off the best "rissolé" slices, and ate heartily.

Once they were fed Garibaldi evinced a desire to return

to the sea and his ship. It was impossible because the fire had spread in that direction. He caught sight, however, of the River Arroga, and they started for it. Beside the river they came upon twenty Indians, who shouted in unison "Ham! Ham!" which meant welcome in their language. Here everything was green and fresh, frogs croaked, their croaking interrupted only by the song of the wip-poor-wick, the nightingale of virgin forests. The Indian chief was a handsome savage of forty or so, picturesquely dressed in mutton hide, and, naturally, wore eagle plumes in his hair; two bison horns were clapped to his forehead. His name was Feh-to-peh-ih, that is Sides of the Eagle. Garibaldi gave him some beads, whereupon the Indians danced for him. A good meal followed. Afterwards Garibaldi witnessed a scalping, then he built a raft, and they floated down the river on it. From then onward they had nothing to eat for several days—not even rattlesnakes.

On the fourth day, weakened by hunger, Garibaldi saw his Indian guide tearing leaves from the branches of a tree, then eating them. He did likewise, and his men ate leaves too. The result was disastrous. The leaves had poisoned them, they could hardly drag themselves along, even the slightest effort became impossible. They collapsed. Their bodies were swollen, their eyes almost sightless, and they practically lost their reason. They lay down under a tree, tried to rise but could not. They thought their end had come. Suddenly they heard voices. Garibaldi alone managed to get on his knees, and waved his cloak. He fell after the effort, yet forced himself on his knees again, waved the cloak, and at last a canoe came towards them. It contained some members of his crew. But for Garibaldi's superhuman effort they in the canoe would never have spotted the men under the tree, who would certainly have perished.

On another occasion he was riding with his men. Fifteen horses were needed in those days for three travellers, therefore they took plenty of horses along. Having reached a forest, it was observed that the unmounted horses in front were becoming nervous; even the ridden horses were agitated. That made it evident that there was a tiger or a jaguar about; and, no mistake, a panther came charging the leading remounts while simultaneously a jaguar jumped on a horse in the rear. The horsemen continued quietly on their journey, leaving one horse to the panther, another to the jaguar.

It was fighting the enemies first of Rio Grande then of Uruguay that provided Garibaldi with most of his adventures. In a battle against the Brazilians he cut a horseman's head off with his sabre. The headless horseman trotted in circles round him for quite a while. With his men, who were by then known as the Italian Legion, he reached during his Uruguayan campaigns an estancia called Estancia del Ladrón, which belonged to a man called Andros, who was on the Uruguayan side, thus an enemy of the Argentine dictator Rosas. Andros had his own legion made up of dogs, Newfoundland dogs, which obeyed military commands, and went through their military drill every day.

Garibaldi and Andros decided to look for the enemy in a low mountain range not far from the estancia. The two men rode at the head of the troop in the company of the dogs. When they came near the mountains they caught sight of an enemy squadron bearing down on them.

"We shall be attacked," said Andros, "but it's only cavalry. Leave them to me. You'll laugh."

They halted near a small wood, cut thick branches, with which they built barricades inside the wood, and behind them they became invisible to the enemy. Garibaldi ordered his men not to shoot before the enemy reached the wood. Thus, when they fired, about thirty enemy horsemen fell off their horses dead or wounded.

"It's my turn," said Andros, who then gave the dogs the order to charge.

The huge dogs attacked. They jumped on the horses, thew off the riders, and once on the ground bit them till they became harmless. The rest of the squadron bolted as fast as the frightened horses could go. Andros ordered his warriors back. "Well done, my children," he said, patting them, and the dogs lay down happily, still licking the blood of the enemy off their chops.

Garibaldi's naval battles were equally ferocious and picturesque.

When in 1845 an enemy squadron blockaded Montevideo, in whose service Garibaldi then was, he became impatient with the Uruguayan Navy, which consisted of three cutters, lying idle and doing nothing to lift the blockade. So he went one evening to the tavern called San José where sailors and suchlike folk gathered, and asked for volunteers.

"I need," he said, "twenty men, and if I find them tomorrow the blockade will be lifted and we'll give chase to the enemy."

The whole tavern rose, all he had to do was to select his volunteers. He ordered a gallon of rum, five kilos of brown sugar, thirty grammes of cinammon, lemon and ginger, and made a real American punch, with the flames reaching the ceiling. They drank till the morning to the success of the expedition.

All Montevideo turned out in the morning to watch the battle to come. They did not watch in vain. Garibaldi was nearly captured by the overwhelming enemy forces, but managed to escape through the enemy line with his small cutter. A big schooner of ten guns followed him to a small bay, where he cast anchor, the schooner remaining at the entrance of the bay. Night fell, and in the dark in small boats he and his men boarded the fine schooner, and after a violent fight lasting for twenty minutes they defeated the enemy. In the morning he who was considered lost reappeared before Montevideo in his imposing prize.

The number of El Diablo's exploits was vast, and incredible though those exploits sound they were the roots of the legend, gave Garibaldi numerous opportunities to develop his gifts as guerrillero, and made him perceive that the incredible and the impossible were more his allies than his enemies.

In far-away London Mazzini printed reports of his achievements in the *Apostolato Popolare*, and had them widely circulated in the English newspapers too. "It was," wrote Jessie White Mario, "at first entirely due to Mazzini and for a time to Mazzini only, that Garibaldi's wonderful career in South America became so thoroughly known that when he returned in 1848 he was regarded as a hero and a mighty man of war."

IV

Two matters of intrinsic importance in his life and career had mighty little to do with Mazzini, though they were of the same importance as getting the reputation of hero and man of war. The first was the red shirt; the second, Anita.

The red shirt came to him in Montevideo, and as it often happens with weighty events, it came to him in a commonplace enough fashion. A firm of merchants in Montevideo was overstocked with red shirts, which, because of the blockade, the firm was unable to dispatch to Buenos Aires to be worn by "saladeros" because red shirts do not show spots of blood. Those red shirts were sold cheap in Montevideo, so Garibaldi, who was perpetually broke, bought some for himself and his legion. It would, one feels, have surprised the good merchant of Montevideo even if he had dreamt that with his cheap goods he was the begetter of a new departure in history.

Anita came while Garibaldi was still in Rio Grande, that is at the Laguna, where he met her. "I had never dreamt of marriage," said Garibaldi, "and had always regarded myself as quite unsuited to being a husband, considering that I had too independent a character, and was moreover irresistibly drawn to a life of adventure." But came a moment when he began to feel extremely lonely, and it was then that he needed a wife. He was thinking of that in 1839 when he looked landward from his cabin in the *Itaparika*. On the promontory of La Barra he saw some pretty girls engaged in domestic work. One of them attracted him more than the rest, so he went ashore with a beating heart, yet with his mind made up. A man invited him into the house wherein the girl dwelt. Garibaldi said to the girl: "Maiden, thou shalt be mine." With those words he had created a bond that death alone could part. Incidentally, the man who asked him in was the maiden's husband.

"But she is dead," he cried to Dumas in 1861, "and he is avenged. When did I recognize the greatness of the fault? There at the mouth of the Eridan, on the day when, hoping to dispute with death, I pressed her pulse convulsively to count its last beats. . . ." (One can sympathize with Dumas when, having read that, he said to Garibaldi: "Read this, my friend, it does not seem clear.")

Anita, Garibaldi's maiden, was a native of Murrinho,

christened Anna Maria, and was the daughter of Bento Ribeiro of São Paolo and of Maria Bento Ribeiro Antunes of Tubarao. She was about twenty years old when she and Garibaldi met. Her husband was Manoel José Duarte of Barra da Logoa, a fisherman whom she had married four years previously. However, that little impediment did not worry the lovers unduly. She left her husband on the spot and sailed away with Garibaldi.

She was, the legend has it, slim, vivacious, pretty and her hair was brown. He married her (continues the legend) in fine weather facing the sun. Warriors' songs were their wedding anthem. At the repast Anita sat next to Garibaldi, who, after the toasts, turned to her and said: "And you, delicate daughter of Laguna, don't you wish to raise your glass too?"

"I raise my glass to the brave defenders of Laguna, and to the brave and generous exiles from Italy, who have come to offer their arms to Rio Grande. Let them find, when the hour of independence of their country strikes, equally generous hearts to help them with their blood and their arms, and let them, led by you, beloved, smash the chains of their country as I smash this glass."

Having delivered herself of that moving toast she smashed to the ground a magnificent crystal tumbler. Henceforward Garibaldi not only loved her but adored her, too. The wedding party continued well into the night.

"There's somebody there," exclaimed Anita, pointing at the undulating high grass, and at that very moment a bullet came whizzing past. Out of the grass rose about fifty men and the battle began, in the course of which Anita killed three men and was lightly wounded in the left shoulder. That was her wedding night.

The truth about Anita is that she was neither slim nor pretty. She was tall and on the fattish side, with prominent hanging breasts, her face oval and freckled all over, eyes and hair black. She was a bit of a shrew. After defeating the army of Oribe in the battle of San Antonio, which was Garibaldi's fiercest in South America, the French admiral Laine went to call on him to congratulate him. On arriving at his house in Montevideo, he pushed the front door open and fell straightway over a chair in the darkness. Garibaldi heard the fracas, and the admiral heard him telling Anita to light a candle.

"How can I?" she screamed. "There's not a penny to buy a candle."

The admiral afterwards related that to the Uruguayan minister of war, who sent a hundred patacoons to Garibaldi, who bought a pound of candles and gave the rest of the money to the widows of his soldiers.

In Montevideo Anita had the reputation of being a heretic of low origin, a shrew given to drink and swearing, and cursing God and the Saints. With the latter her always abstemious lover could not have disagreed.

The Brazilians around 1839 had a song of seven verses about the well-matched pair, all very amusing, but let us quote only two.

> Garibaldi na Italia
> Só comia macarrão
> Ao chegar cá no Brasil,
> Carne seca com feijão.

(In Italy Garibaldi ate macaroni, on arrival in Brazil lean meat with dry beans.)

> A mulher de Garibaldi
> E uma santa mulher;
> Nos domingos vai à missa
> E volta à noite quando quer.

(Garibaldi's wife is a saintly woman; on Sundays goes to Mass and comes back at night when she feels like it.)

3

In 1842 they heard a rumour that her husband was dead, so she and Garibaldi got married in the church of St Francis of Assisi in Montevideo. She became a jealous wife, and Giuseppe Guerzoni, her husband's faithful secretary and probably best biographer, mentioned as an extenuating circumstance that the poor creole woman suffered from a sense of inferiority because she was neither good to look at nor educated, almost a savage, and therefore felt far beneath her extremely handsome and famous husband. All the women who cheered and adulated the hero of battles were for her just women who were after her man.

One day Garibaldi appeared before his legionaries with his flowing mane and beard cut short. "How could you?" was the cry. "Cosa volete," replied Garibaldi, and one can almost see him shrugging his shoulder, "my wife is jealous and believes I carry my hair long to please other women. She has tormented me so much over my accursed locks that I, for peace in the home, had them cut off."

There were, one has to admit, plenty of reasons for any woman to be jealous of Garibaldi, who was a lustful man. In defence of his sexual escapades Guerzoni maintained that not even to Garibaldi could Nature give every perfection, and praises him for never behaving in an underhand manner in such matters; on the contrary, he operated in broad daylight. "I love you, you appeal to me, I want you," he would say to women, and if they agreed, which undoubtedly many of them did, he, beast of prey but never of fraud, clasped them in his arms; and if a woman repulsed him he did not take it to heart; speaking of a relation thwarted in love the great man exclaimed: "Frankly, I cannot understand it. To die for a woman when the world is so full of them! What stupidity! I say to women: 'You love me? I love you. Don't you love me? Worse for you.'"

Nevertheless, Anita he incorporated into his legend, and once inside it she stayed there for good. Long after her death he still spoke of her as the greatest, finest, bravest woman he had known and loved, and turned her into a martyr of Italy with all the paraphernalia that went with it.

Besides, he did not mind a woman being a shrew and he had nothing against fat, uneducated women with big hanging breasts. Though duchesses and other refined women came to adore him, his true taste in women remained in harmony for his whole life with the requirements of the Old Port of Nice. A rich English lady would want to marry him; a romantic bluestocking like Mme Schwartz could chase him; but with all good will and friendship towards them he would abed with some hefty servant girl from his native Nice and love the children she would produce for him. As in other matters, so in sex, success never turned Garibaldi's head.

Anita was certainly the right wife for a guerrillero. She went with him into battle like any of his men, and when he ordered her in a naval engagement to go below, "If I do," she said, "it will be but to drive out those cowards who have sought concealment down there." Not very feminine, but admirable words for a warrior's warrior woman. In another battle near the town of Coritibani she was taken prisoner, managed to escape and rode across a wilderness of sixty miles to rejoin Garibaldi. "In short," said Bent, "the stories of Anita's life, if collected into a volume, would equal in romance any of the backwoods stories which schoolboys devour with avidity. . . . Why has Mayne Reid passed over so suitable a heroine for his tales?"

Anita gave birth wellnigh on horseback to four children, two boys and two girls. The first-born was Menotti, called after the credulous martyr of Modena. Menotti became a worthy, noisy lieutenant of his father, as endowed with lack of physical fear as his progenitor. The second son was called Ricciotti, after another martyr, another fearless man. The elder of the two girls, Teresa, grew into a woman of a formidable personality and married a Genoese lawyer, Stefano Canzio, whose beliefs were even more radical and anticlerical, if possible, than her father's; the second daughter, Rosita, died tragically. The child and her nurse were burnt to death in bed before succour came and the locked door could be opened. Her death haunted Garibaldi throughout his life, and when some visitor came to the old General on his island of Caprera and, staying the night, wanted to lock his door, he would say: "What do you fear in the house of Garibaldi that makes you lock your door?"

It is difficult to conceive how, with four children, Anita managed to go on fighting in battles, yet she did, and at the time she was taken prisoner she plunged a knife into the sentry's neck, killing him instantaneously. She was against their leaving her native land, and was not pleased when they removed to Montevideo, where Garibaldi in the beginning earned his living as a commercial traveller, his samples ranging from Italian *pasta* to Rouen textiles. Later on he taught mathematics, but soon he was in the midst of fighting again with his Italian legion, and, as mentioned before, his outstanding victory was the battle of Salto San Antonio, which, experts have it, deserves to rank with Calatafimi and Milazzo.

V

Italy was getting ready, as it were, for Garibaldi. The idea of a united Italy had been brought to Italy by Napoleon I, and after 1815 the idea was kept alive by the Carbonaria, followed by Mazzini's Young Italy, to which should be added the dynastic aspirations of the House of Savoy. But the fateful hour had not struck yet for Charles Albert of Savoy-Carignan, King of Sardinia, that is of Piedmont. Only conspiracies kept the idea alive, and they could at times be movingly childish. In January 1821, for example, Austrian troops marched through Modena on their way to Naples. Anonymous tracts were distributed among the Hungarian soldiers in the Austrian contingent. The tracts were in Latin. Though it was unlikely that the simple Hungarian soldiers could have understood any Latin, the Duke of Modena had thirty of his subjects arrested.

Childish too, though far more dangerous, were Mazzini's conspiracies, the most unsuccessful of which was the attempt of the Bandiera brothers, Attilio and Emilio. On 11th June 1844 they embarked with eighteen companions in Corfu for a landing in Calabria in the Kingdom of Naples. (Austria knew of their movements, thanks to intercepted letters between Mazzini and the brothers. Lord Aberdeen's administration was blamed for tampering with the letters at the Post Office.) They landed near Cotrone, knelt down, kissed the soil and said: "Thou hast given us life; we give our lives to thee." Among them was an unfrocked priest, Boccheciampi, a traitor, whom, however, nobody suspected because he had been to England where he loudly declared his patriotic sentiments. He sent at once secret information to the governor of Otranto, then vanished.

The patriots waited in vain for insurgents to come to their aid. Instead of them Neapolitan troops arrived. (Here one can see why Garibaldi would have no time for conspiracies but only for *coups de main*.) In the course of the engagement two of the patriots were killed, three, including Emilio Bandiera, were wounded, and all were taken to Cosenza. They refused to have counsel at their trial, except for three they were all sentenced to death, and at dawn on 25th July were led to the Vallone di Rovito, singing the chorus of Donna Caritea: "Chi per la patria muore vissuto ha assai" (He who dies for his country has lived long enough). The soldiers fired badly. "Courage," shouted Ricciotti, after whom Garibaldi's son would be named, to the soldiers. "Do your duty. We too are soldiers." They died only after the third volley, but till the end shouted "Viva Italia!" The disastrous attempt was not in vain since, so Mazzini said, Italy needed martyrs.

Martyrs alone cannot push out the foreigner. The foreigner in Italy at that time was Austria, and to her belonged Milan and Venice. The duchies of Parma and Modena and the Grand Duchy of Tuscany were under Austria's armed protection. Metternich considered Italy but as a geographical expression, and with that he defined the Habsburg dynasty's attitude towards its possessions. For the Emperor in Vienna Milan and Venice were part and parcel of the Habsburg dominions. National aspirations were alien to the dynasty. The Italian territories were on the same level as, say, Bohemia or Croatia. They were theirs, and you hold on to your belongings because they belong to you. Therefore the true *straniero*, that is foreigner, was Austria, and it is ironical indeed that when the Italians were not helped by the French, they were, between 1848–66, every time smartly defeated by the foreigner.

South of the Austrian possessions, and what today would be called her satellites, extended the Papal State and, south of it, the Kingdom of the Two Sicilies, certainly an Italian state ruled by the Bourbons of Naples. The Bourbons were reactionaries, considered constitutions as something to be given when things went against them, and to be taken back at the first opportunity. Their rule was despotic, or rather they based their rule on despotism. Mr Gladstone was to expose the horrors of the Neapolitan system, nevertheless it was an Italian state insofar as it was neither ruled nor held by foreigners.

It was in the centre, namely, in the Papal State, that the hope and light of Italian Union became tangible for the first time since 1815. And the man who gave the hope and the light was Giovanni Maria Mastai Ferretti, elevated to the Papal Throne as Pius IX in 1846, the same Pio Nono on whose coffin in 1881 the Roman populace hurled mud as it was carried for final burial to the church of San Lorenzo fuori le Mure. Pio Nono at the time of his elevation was known as a liberal. (A good Italian he remained till death.) Gregory XVI had said: "In his household everybody is liberal—even his cat."

On his elevation Pio Nono began at once to carry out his reforms with great love and zeal. He was influenced by Gioberti's *Del primato morale e civile degli Italiani*, whose argument was that since the west had been civilized by Italy through the Church, the Church was a greater asset to Italy than revolution. Besides, the Pope with his temporal possessions was also an Italian prince, and if Italy wanted to become united the Italian states should federate under the presidency of the Pope. Though Mazzini's Italy was one indivisible republic, one cannot but reflect that if such a confederacy had come about Mazzini would have found his God and People-sent opportunity to bring it down from within.

At any rate he started his work from within soon after the Pope proclaimed a general amnesty, reformed the administration, the judicature and the financial system. The exiles who came back were mostly Mazzinians, the now unmolested press and clubs that sprang up in Rome were Mazzinian, and Mazzini himself wrote a somewhat condescending letter to Pio Nono. "There is no man, I will not say in Italy but in Europe more powerful than you. You have, therefore, most blessed father, immense duties. . . . To fulfil the mission which God entrusts to you two things are necessary: to believe, and to unify Italy." (It is a recurring impression that those engaged in the Risorgimento often forgot that Catholics existed outside Italy. The Pope was the Pope of the faithful even if many of them had nothing to do with unifying Italy.)

In those days of enthusiasm for the new Pope, Pio Nono received a letter from somebody else too, a letter that came the whole way from Montevideo via the Nuncio in Brazil.

MOST ILLUSTRIOUS AND VENERABLE SEIGNEUR.

From the moment when we received the first news of the exaltation of the Sovereign Pontiff Pius IX, and of the amnesty he was granting to the poor conscripts, we have, with an ever increasing attention and interest, been following the imprint of the steps which the Supreme Head of the Church is leaving on the path of glory and liberty. . . .

We who are writing to you, most illustrious and venerable Seigneur, are men who—ever animated by that passion which has made us face exile—have taken up arms at Montevideo in support of a cause that appeared to us to be just. We have gathered round us some hundreds of our fellow countrymen who had come hither in the hope of finding less troublous times than those they had to endure in their own country. . . .

If then, at the present moment, the assistance of our men, who are not unfamiliar with the bearing of arms, is accepted by His Holiness, needless to say that ever so much more willingly should we consecrate our labours to the service of one who is doing so much for his country and the Church. So we shall deem ourselves happy if we can come to the aid of the redemptive work of Pius IX, and we shall not consider

that we are paying too dear a price for the privilege if it be
with the blood of us all. . . .

"Tempora," remarked Mme Schwartz when quoting
part of the letter, "mutantur." She had probably met in
Caprera Garibaldi's donkey named Pio Nono. That
donkey, however, came into Garibaldi's life many years
after the letter was written and remained unanswered. It is
purely food for speculation to ask oneself what would
have happened if the Pope had accepted the proffered
sword. Garibaldi might have been faithful to him, provided he personally liked him, till 29th April 1848 when in
his allocution to the cardinals the Pope proclaimed his
neutrality in the war against Austria, which was not, after
all, strange considering that the Austrians were over-
whelmingly Roman Catholics. After the proclamation
Garibaldi would certainly have defected, would have
fought the Austrians with or without the Papal general
Durando, and would just as certainly have turned up in
Rome to offer his sword to the Roman Republic. That
"if" of history would hardly have made any difference.

The enthusiasm for the liberal Pope and the constitution
found no echo in Metternich. "Each day," he wrote to
Count Apponyi, the Austrian Ambassador in Rome,
"the Pope shows himself more lacking in any practical
sense. Born and brought up in a *liberal* family, he has been
formed in a bad school; a good priest, he has never turned
his mind towards matters of government. Warm of heart
and weak of intellect, he has allowed himself to be taken
and ensnared. . . ." Metternich prophesied that the Pope
would, if matters followed their natural course, be driven
out of Rome.

Soon the enthusiasm shifted from Rome to Piedmont.
Charles Albert had been for a long time under a cloud in

the eyes of Young Italy for having betrayed the Carbonaria, so they asserted, in 1821. Now, however, he was preparing for war against Austria, which would cost him his throne. During a demonstration in Genoa young Nino Bixio, who would become a hero of the Risorgimento and of the Thousand, and in the distant future the king's general who would take Rome, placed his hand on Charles Albert's carriage and shouted to him: "Sire, cross the Tessin and we will follow you to death!" Commenting on it, Mazzini remarked there was too much childishness in Italy. Yesterday it was "Viva Pio Nono!", now it was "Viva Carlo Alberto!", and tomorrow it may be "Viva the Grand Duke of Tuscany!" Yet, he reflected, it was well that those things were, they could only lead to good. And Charles Albert proudly declared to Count de la Tour: "L'Italia si farà da se."

Meanwhile far from all the wheels within wheels Garibaldi decided to leave Montevideo and return to Italy with a part of his legion. Unbeknown to him, his hour was approaching. His vague idea was to go to the assistance of the revolution wherever he may find it, and to kindle its fires. He was thinking of rousing the revolution among the Abruzzesi, for example. The point was that he was leaving because the hour had struck without him having seen the clock or heard the chimes.

Lack of money was the trouble once more. He overcame that by opening a subscription among the Italians in the Oriental Republic of Uruguay. His compatriots put their hands into their pockets, but on his own admission there was an opposition which did its best to frighten his legionaries, predicting certain death if they followed Garibaldi. The fate of the brothers Bandiera, said the chicken-hearted, would be their fate too. It probably would have been their fate if events out of Garibaldi's control had not come, as it were, to the rescue; and that would happen again and again with Garibaldi, whose lucky star undoubtedly was busy, constant and efficient. Had there been no war in 1848 in Italy, and had he really landed in the Abruzzi to rouse the populace to rebellion, he too might have ended his life before a firing squad; and though it is anticipating, it was again luck that made his landing in Sicily possible in 1860. Still luck is part and parcel of greatness. Without luck it could go unseen.

The subscription to help him and his friends to leave Uruguay was aided by the grateful government, but all he accepted from the government were two cannons and eight hundred muskets. When the moment of departure came the captain of the brig *Biponte Carolo* extorted so much money from Garibaldi and his companions that some of them had to stay in bed during the voyage because they had to sell even their shirts, which, we take it, were red. Of the eighty-five who promised to follow Garibaldi only fifty-six embarked with him. Anita and his three children accompanied him.

His friend Anzani, who had signed the letter to the Pope with him, was slowly dying of disease during the voyage. Anita nursed him, and on reaching the Mediterranean they sailed up to Palo, about five miles from Alicante, where they went ashore to buy a goat and oranges for the sick man. Garibaldi heard from the Sardinian vice-consul for the first time that the Piedmontese Constitution had been proclaimed; that the people of Turin ran to the royal palace singing the hymn "Pio Nono"; that Lombardy and Venice were up in arms; and that the Milanese had driven the Austrians out on 23rd March. In short, the fat was in the fire.

The vice-consul told him of the revolutions in Paris, Berlin and Vienna, and probably the most surprising tiding was that Ferdinand of Naples had promised his subjects a constitution. Garibaldi had met his hour, and on his return to the brig the Sardinian flag was hoisted by the quondam deserter, who was still under sentence of death.

His friends were against his landing in Nice because of the death sentence; but as such trifles did not worry Garibaldi he steered the brig to Nice, where they landed with him on 24th June 1848 after fourteen years of absence. He took Anita and the children to his mother, the priest-ridden old woman, who according to some did not treat Anita kindly. Somehow one cannot imagine the shrew of the Pampas being bullied by the pious old woman, of whom Garibaldi was inordinately fond, though they had many arguments about religion, which did not stop the old woman from sending her grandchildren to the Jesuit school when the parents were away.

VI

Garibaldi decided that he would offer his sword to Charles Albert, because, as he put it, he was ready to place his sword "at the service of whatsoever Italian prince would use it for Italy". Apparently Charles Albert was that prince for the moment. He ceased to be that prince when he received Garibaldi coldly, which was not surprising considering the little business of desertion and high treason. The king was courteous during their meeting, though naturally enough, was not taken by the subject who had tried to bring about a mutiny in his ship the *Eurydice*. Not to like Garibaldi was already a sin in Garibaldi's eyes.

"I saw him," he said of his audience, "saw the man who had executed Italy's noblest sons, who had condemned me and so many others to death, and I understood the coldness of his reception, and yet I would have served Italy under a king, as under a republic." Then comes one of those irritating judgments, irritating because totally unfair, of which Garibaldi was pastmaster. "I will not now uplift the stone that covers a tomb," he said of the man who had risked all for Italy, lost all and died of a broken heart, "nor criticize conduct that must be judged by posterity . . . to head the war of Independence, he did not respond to the confidence reposed in him."

Garibaldi was told to go to the minister of war in Turin; he had already been advised to go and ply his trade of corsair in the Adriatic. His friend Giacomo Medici, though angry with him for having gone to see the king, took Garibaldi to Milan; and here one should stop to take a look at Garibaldi before he meets the provisional government of Lombardy.

He was already forty-one years old, and except for the stillborn *Eurydice* mutiny he had achieved nothing in Italy yet. But now he was the home-town boy who had made good. The author, who spent several years of his boyhood and adolescence in Italy, often saw there returned, successful Italian emigrants from America, walking with a swagger and a gold watch chain. In Garibaldi's case the gold watch chain was his renown in South America: in lieu of an ice-cream parlour or a spaghetti shop he possessed the laurels of audacious attacks and brilliant victories. His fame, chiefly owing to Mazzini, had preceded him, and in those days it was balm indeed for Italians to be able to number among themselves a brave condottiere. Italian military exploits were still of the future: the military past was far back, dim, and centuries lay fallow between past and present. They were not far wrong who said it was Garibaldi who in Rio Grande and Uruguay gave Italy her military tradition.

Garibaldi was perfectly aware of all that. In the land of hombres he had been looked upon as an extraordinarily fine hombre. Did not he defeat hombres by the score, and did not he in the world of hombres take an hombre's wife away? And did not the Italian exiles flock to his flag and fight and conquer under him? He was entitled to the gold watch chain.

South America had given him the conviction that he was a better soldier than anybody else. He had no sense of humour, thus doubts could not assail him, and since he was given to bombastic speech and laying down the law, it was a good thing for him, and perhaps for Italy too, that he had not the gift of laughing at himself. This does not mean that if one has a sense of humour one does not talk nonsense: it simply implies that the nonsense one talks is less convincing if one has it.

Garibaldi's was a hedged-in mind, and a simple mind at that. If thoughts have colour, then his were purple where himself, Italy and his devotees were concerned, and an angry yellow when he thought of his enemies, who became for him invariably the enemies of Italy too. If Italy meant God and the People to Mazzini, then one could say that Italy for Garibaldi was Italy and Garibaldi together. Almost all worshippers, devotees and followers who met him referred to his modesty. Modest he was. His was the insufferable modesty of one who is so sure of himself, so satisfied with himself that he takes his greatness for granted and finds it unnecessary to have recourse to boasting, apologizing or even explaining. All that played a vital part in making him an exceptional leader and warrior.

Edward Dicey, an English observer of the Risorgimento, a shrewd man, though with an admittedly Cavourian bias, after remarking no Italian could speak the truth about Garibaldi (he knew what he was speaking about) summed him up as follows: Garibaldi was a man of courage, great physical energy, with the wonderful art of winning over, though not of influencing, all with whom he came into contact. He sprang from the people, he had an instinctive power of appealing to the people's energies, was the perfect guerrilla hero. He had no political education, no knowledge of the principles of government, and was devoid of that rough sharpness which often serves uneducated men in lieu of hating. A warm friend, a bitter hater, he judged political affairs by his own prepossessions. Without power of appreciating character or of withstanding flattery he was fooled by many whom ordinary prudence should have taught him to distrust.

Dicey admitted that if Garibaldi were greater his influence would possibly be less. The fact that his ideas were limited and that his mind was not able to grasp more than one side of a question gave him that concentration of purpose and intensity of faith necessary to form a popular leader. His very weaknesses and affectation endeared him to the common people as much as his virtues.

Thus was Garibaldi described by a past president (1850) of the Cambridge Union.

Another Englishman, the already quoted Theodore Bent, admired Garibaldi for remaining throughout simple and unaffected, and considered him great, good and guilty; great because he had done great things, and had the simplicity and tenderness of soul that belongs to greatness; good inasmuch as he had lived amongst corrupt people, was brought into contact with every species of corruption, yet his public life was not stained by one single blot of that sort; and guilty because in his obstinacy and wilfulness he had set at nought and maligned with unmitigated abuse men who had, with the same object in view, expressed views different to his own, and because he was from time to time the advocate of anarchy and rebellion. (His advocacy of anarchy and his atheism irked many of his English friends.)

George Sand, who came to consider Mazzini, in modern parlance, not pink enough for her liking, said of Garibaldi: "Qui ne ressemble à personne, et il y a en lui une sorte de mystère, qui fait réfléchir."

Garibaldi was a heavy-boned man, his waist narrow, his hips wide, so he could wear trousers without a belt. A lot of fuss was made of his Christ-like appearance. Perhaps the beard was responsible for that; certainly not the cunning eyes. Be that as it may, Garibaldi and his associates cashed in on it, and there was circulated, for instance, in 1850 a lithograph representing him as our Lord, circulated for the benefit of the simple Italian peasants. He was not over-tall, his arms and legs moved with a slow rhythm, and his was the walk of the sailor.

That was the man who, with Giacomo Medici, set out for Milan, and Milan in 1848 was a pretty kettle of fish. The Milanese had driven out the Austrians during the Five Days—18th–22nd March—then established a provisional government, and on 7th April Mazzini appeared in Milan. He was received with great effusion, and a torchlight procession escorted him to the Hotel della Bella Venezia, and in the course of the following days he spoke eloquently to the Milanese, urging them to drive the *straniero* out of Italy. Acting in a more practical manner, Charles Albert crossed the Ticino with the Piedmontese army. In his first battle he routed the Austrians at Monte Chiaro. Soon, however, the Milanese expressed their disappointment at the king being unable to cut off the retreat of the Austrians to the Quadrilateral (the fortresses of Mantua, Peschiera, Legnano, and Verona).

The Milanese were convinced that it was the king's fault.

They were convinced too that Turin was jealous of Milan because Milan was, according to the Milanese, a fitter town for a capital than Turin. The Turinese thought, of course, the opposite. The Milanese missed the point. The point was that a man from the eighteenth century had come to halt, even if only for eleven years, the progress of the nineteenth. The man was the Austrian field-marshal Joseph, Count von Radetzky, who was born in 1766 and had fought for the first time in Italy in the year 1796 against Napoleon Bonaparte. Once he had the necessary re-inforcements he would erupt from the Quadrilateral, and at the age of eighty-two defeat the Italians at Custozza, and at the age of eighty-three would crown his long military career by the victory of Novara, defeating the Italians again.

The Milanese had special reasons to dislike the aged warrior. In January 1848 a tract was distributed in Milan calling on the Milanese to stop smoking, so that the Austrians should not be paid the cigar tax. The Milanese boycotted tobacco most patriotically, and old Radetzky distributed thirty thousand cigars among his troops, ordering them to smoke them in the streets and blow the smoke into the faces of passers-by. Whether the good citizens considered it a provocation or were tantalized by the cigar smell, we know not; but Radetzky's cigars caused riots, which resulted in five dead, including the podestà, and about fifty wounded.

The provisional government of Lombardy believed more in politics than in organizing a purely Lombard army, consequently the Piedmontese ran the whole war show, and their army occupied Novara, Mortara and Voghera, and seized the powder magazine of Peschiera in the Quadrilateral. They moved against Castelnuovo, where the Austrians surprised and defeated them. The Lombard government was incapable of feeding the Piedmontese army, which did not help matters either, and sooner or later Pio Nono would be blamed too for Radetzky out-generalling Charles Albert. The Pope's declaration of neutrality would be used as an excuse for the defeat at Custozza, yet in that fluid year of 1848 not only did the Papal forces come to the aid of Piedmont, but even the Neapolitans lumbered up from the south; meanwhile Radetzky effected junction with Generals d'Aspre and Nugent. The provisional government in Milan decided on annexing Lombardy to Piedmont while in Turin con-fidence prevailed. Austria was a phantom and Radetzky's army a shadow. Politics were still judged more important than defeating the Austrians. In circular letters to all provisional governments Charles Albert asked for the convocation of constitutional assemblies. That was putting the cart before the horse; for the war was not going well. The Piedmontese were repulsed from Verona, and instead of attacking General Nugent they went to lay siege to Peschiera, thus allowing Radetzky to increase his forces. True that Prince Turn und Taxis was heavily beaten at Vicenza by the Venetian volunteers and the Papal army of General Durando, but Nugent had reached Radetzky; true too that on 29th May the Austrians were defeated by the Piedmontese general Brava, but then came the Austrian counter-attack taking back Vicenza, Treviso and Palmanuevo, and Charles Albert, who had the besieging of the strong fortress of Mantua in mind, was accused of doing nothing and wasting his time on the right bank of the Adige. Radetzky was building up his forces for the great onslaught, while the Venetian cities were lost and in Milan verbal battles raged between the fusionists and the non-fusionists. Colonel Forbes, another Englishman, saw the situation clearly. "While Radetzky was collecting bayonets," he wrote, "Charles Albert was collecting votes." Garibaldi, who did not care much for votes but believed implicitly in bayonets, would heartily have agreed with him.

Years later, looking back in New York on his arrival in Milan in 1848, Garibaldi complained of his reception there. (Mazzini said he was not to be blamed for that: quite the contrary; it was he who had acquainted the Milanese with Garibaldi's brave exploits in South America.) The provisional government did not want to give him arms, but gave him the rank of general and authorized him to raise battalions of Lombard volunteers. He was always an excellent recruiting sergeant for Garibaldi. Whereas Mazzini appealed to brains, Garibaldi went straight for the man, sucking him into the warmth of his passion and self-assurance. In no time he raised in the unknown —to him—town of Vicenza a battalion of volunteers. Mazzini was left to carry for a few days their standard inscribed with "Dio e Popolo". The provisional ministry of war refused uniforms, so the volunteers took linen uniforms left behind by the Austrian troops, and made blouses of them. Medici said that in those blouses they looked like a regiment of cooks. Then somehow they procured arms. Garibaldi was not the man to waste time, and off he marched his volunteers to Bergamo. They were recalled to Milan. When they reached Monza on their march back they heard that Milan had capitulated to Radetzky. Now a wise ordinary man would have disbanded his volunteers, since the war was pretty well lost. Not so Garibaldi. He ordered his volunteers to march on Como. He had his men, therefore he wanted to fight, but fight as near as possible to the Swiss frontier to be able to cross over if the necessity arose.

At Como there were plenty of desertions. Out of the

five thousand volunteers only eight hundred were left. The others went to Switzerland. From Como Garibaldi moved to La Camerlata, from there he retired on San Fermo, where he addressed his men, telling them he wanted to carry on guerrilla warfare, and pointed out to them that it was the least dangerous mode of fighting. Nevertheless, about four hundred more volunteers deserted. (Garibaldi must have seen himself and his men somewhere on the pampas, and not in thickly inhabited Northern Italy with a huge professional army coming against him.) He refused to return to Piedmont, marched on to Castelletto on the Ticino, then sent Medici to bring back as many deserters as he could. Medici calmly took himself as far as Lugano in Switzerland, bringing back about three hundred men. Now it appeared to Garibaldi that he had sufficient men to fight Austria, but before taking to fighting he proclaimed Charles Albert a traitor to Italy, and said it was the duty of every Italian patriot to make war against the Italian king of Piedmont.

Giulio Dandolo, who was with that strange tiny army, gave this description of it:

> ... an incongruous assemblage of individuals of all descriptions: boys of twelve and fourteen, veteran soldiers attracted by the fame of the celebrated chieftain of Montevideo; some stimulated by ambition, others seeking for impunity and licence in the confusion of war, yet so restrained by the inflexible severity of their leader, that courage and daring alone could find vent, while more lawless passions were curbed beneath his will. The General and his staff all rode on American saddles, wore scarlet blouses with hats of every possible form, without distinction of any kind, or pretension to military ornament. Followed by their orderlies, most of whom had come from America, they might be seen hurrying to and fro, now dispersing, then again collecting—active, rapid and in-

defatigable. Garibaldi, if the encampment was far from the scene of danger, would stretch himself under his tent; if on the contrary the enemy was near at hand, he remained constantly on horseback, giving orders, and visiting outposts. Often disguised as a peasant he risked his own safety in daring reconnaissances. . . . When the General's trumpet gave the signal for departure, lassos secured the horses, which had been left to graze in the meadows. . . . Garibaldi appeared more like the chief of a tribe of Indians than a general; but at the approach of danger and in the heat of combat his presence of mind was admirable; and then by the astonishing rapidity of his movements he made up in great measure for his deficiency in those qualities which are generally supposed to be absolutely essential to a military commander.

Dandolo should have added that with "the astonishing rapidity of his movements" Garibaldi had another advantage over military commanders, namely he could make himself and his troops vanish, which would enable him to claim victory where a professional soldier would admit defeat.

Having declared Charles Albert a traitor Garibaldi took his men to Arona, where he seized two lake steamers. The band of volunteers embarked, and the steamers paddled to Luino. Garibaldi was feverish, went into an inn and lay down. Medici promised his sleep would not be disturbed. Austria willed it otherwise. Half an hour later a peasant Medici had sent out to scout, came back shouting: "The Austrians, the Austrians!"

Though Garibaldi was in high fever he jumped out of bed, rushed out of the inn, divided his force into two columns. The Austrians came marching along the high road and took the inn. Garibaldi ordered one of the columns to attack the inn. The Austrians numbered about twelve hundred, but that did not deter Garibaldi. When he saw that the column was not able to dislodge the Austrians he threw the second column against the inn too. After an assault with bayonets in the garden the Garibaldians put the Austrians to flight. Garibaldi sent Medici in pursuit of the fleeing enemy. With his company consisting only of a hundred men owing to the desertions, Medici threw himself after the Austrians, who ran too fast for him.

News came in the night that another Austrian corps was marching on them. Garibaldi ordered Medici to hold Germiniada. Barricades were erected and battlements formed on the houses. Thanks to their South American experiences with that type of fortification the work was done in an hour. News came that the Austrians were not approaching. Garibaldi dispatched three companies in different directions. On their return he sent them on Guerla, from Guerla they moved on Varese, where the population gave them a rousing welcome. A spy was caught and Garibaldi had him shot. They were, Medici proudly tells us, advancing straight against Radetzky. For Radetzky the whole affair was just a tiny sideshow.

The Austrians' plan was to put themselves between Switzerland and Garibaldi, and to achieve that they sent out three columns. Medici took his own column against them, prepared to fight, but to fight under the most favourable conditions, that is as near to the Swiss frontier as possible. He seized three villages—Catzone, Ligurno and Rodero—which not only guarded the roads leading from Como, but "I had only, so to speak, to roll down in order to find myself in Switzerland—that is to say on neutral territory". The Austrians attacked Rodero, which they found deserted. The Garibaldian garrison had rolled down into Switzerland in the course of the night. During his encounter with the Austrians Medici fought in front of spectators; for a number of Swiss had appeared on the

mountainside to watch the engagement. Medici hoped in
vain that Garibaldi would come to his rescue. Garibaldi
was otherwise engaged. So Medici, as he puts it, maintained his position against the Austrians till his last cart-
ridge was spent, then gathered his men and took them to
Switzerland. He was furious when he heard that the
Austrian general d'Aspre dared to claim the engagement
as a victory.

In Lugano Medici received news of Garibaldi, whose
line of retreat to Switzerland had been cut by d'Aspre.
That did not discourage Garibaldi, who wanted to squeeze
what juice remained out of his private war against the
foreigner. He went to Morazzone where he encamped,
was immediately surrounded by five thousand Austrians,
fought them with his five hundred men all day long,
charged them after darkness, and having bayoneted his
way through he and his men reached open country again.
His next move was to dismiss his men, give them a
rendezvous in Lugano, and off he went to Switzerland.
The private war was over.

When Medici went to see him near Lugano he was in
bed, dead tired and almost unable to speak. Yet he asked
at once: "Have you your company ready?" Medici
assured him that his company was ready. "Very well,"
said Garibaldi. "Let me sleep this one night; tomorrow
we will rally our men and start afresh." Though Garibaldi
was up and about on the next day even he perceived that
for the moment he could not start afresh. He returned to
Piedmont and went to Genoa.

The real war, namely Charles Albert's war, ended on
24th July at Custozza. He was thoroughly beaten by
Radetzky, and had to fall back on Milan. The Milanese
turned on him, and he was literally besieged in the Palazzo
Greppi. On 5th August he surrendered Milan to the

Austrians. An armistice was arranged and, deeply distressed, the unlucky monarch went home from war to Turin. General della Rocca, who saw him on the day the Milanese howled outside the Palazzo Greppi, noticed how deathly pale he was and aged in face and figure. He held his sword tight under his arm and said to the general: "Ah, mon cher La Rocca, quelle journée, quelle journée!"

Garibaldi thus commented on the unfortunate king: "If he chooses to preserve his crown by dint of crime and cowardice, we will not abandon our sacred soil to the profanation of the usurpers." He said that shortly before crossing into Switzerland.

The criminal and the coward made one last noble heroic attempt for Italy. On 12th March in the following year he denounced the armistice with Austria, and took the field with an army of sixty-five thousand men. He gave the command to a Polish general called Chrzanowski. Radetzky was the opponent. The Austrians were seventy thousand strong with a hundred and eighty-two guns; Charles Albert had a hundred and forty. Chrzanowski took the king's army to Magenta: the enemy was not there. He heard that the Austrians were at Pavia: he marched his army back to Vigevano. Radetzky appeared swiftly on the scene, cutting off Ramorino's Sardinian division south of the Po. A battle was fought at Mortara, and the Sardinians were pushed back to Novara. There the Pole decided to await Radetzky; and Radetzky came, and with one army corps, without waiting for reinforcements, the old man of eighty-three fell on the entire Piedmontese army, totally defeating it before sunset. Charles Albert abdicated that night in favour of his sturdy son Victor Emmanuel II, who would gather the rose where his father found only the thorn. Charles Albert left his country, and retired to a monastery in Oporto. He died of a broken heart on 28th July. Garibaldi did not change his opinion of him.

Count Cavour, who had witnessed the war as a journalist, and whom Garibaldi would hate with equal hatred and malice, summed up Novara thus: "We have lost thousands of brave soldiers; we have wasted many millions; . . . and from all this we have reaped one single thing: we have got the Italian tricolor as our standard instead of the flag of Savoy. Well, in my opinion we have not paid too dear a price."

VII

From Switzerland Garibaldi, as we know, went to Nice. Reunited with his family he spent some time getting rid of a fever. It must have irked him to stay inactive while resistance continued against the foreigner. The resistance was Daniele Manin's in Venice. Garibaldi and Manin never had much to do with each other, but if they had, one could almost take it for granted that Garibaldi would not have got on with him. When he began to feel better Garibaldi left Nice for Genoa where he was offered a command in the regular Sardinian army. Unwilling to change his mind about Charles Albert, he rejected the offer. Soon he would be fighting against the Pope, to whom he had offered his sword too. It was not planned by him: it was brought about by circumstances like everything else in his career.

In Genoa he first toyed with the idea of leading volunteers against the Austrians in the Veneto. He was invariably a magnet for volunteers; in Genoa he collected about two hundred and fifty. The idea of moving against the Austrians he exchanged for a plan to land in Sicily and fight the Neapolitans. To fight the Bourbons was as much an *idée fixe* with him as marching on Rome. He embarked on a

French ship, the *Pharamond*, with his volunteers and sailed
for Leghorn, the first stop on his intended descent on Sicily.
The *Pharamond* entered the port of Leghorn on 25th
October 1848.

The authorities of Leghorn were not altogether happy
to see him and his band. Yet he was well received by them.
They could not cold-shoulder a man who had become
already a legendary hero, and who, incorporated, as it
were, the military virtues the Italians craved for. Garibaldi
was loudly cheered when he stepped ashore and a huge
crowd accompanied him from harbour to city. It was
suggested to him that he should offer his services to the
new Tuscan government in lieu of continuing on his
voyage against Sicily. Garibaldi was willing to think it
over if the government accepted whatever conditions he
made. A telegram was sent to Florence informing the
government that Garibaldi, though still intending to go
to Sicily, would not be averse to considering any offer the
ministers might make, and would be ready to go to
Florence at once. Before there was time for a reply to
arrive another telegram was dispatched to Florence asking
for an urgent decision on Garibaldi's presence in Leghorn.
The answer from Florence was a request for Garibaldi to
wait a little because the government was not constituted
yet. Garibaldi not being the man to bow to delay and to
governments constituted or otherwise, one of the two
governors of Leghorn, Menichetti, took train to Florence
to press the government for a decision; and thirteen
minutes after the train's departure another telegram was
sent to the government. "The people of Leghorn wish
Garibaldi to remain in service of Tuscany . . . must have
definite reply at once. The population is out of hand."

And Garibaldi was angry. He had given them till 7
p.m., yet no definite offer had come by that time. So he

himself telegraphed to Florence asking for a yes or no. At six minutes past eight, still the same evening, a telegram arrived from Florence asking Garibaldi to be patient till the ministry was formed. Seventeen minutes later Florence telegraphed again, and that telegram was followed by one from Menichetti, who had spoken to Montanelli of the ministry in formation, and who confirmed what he had telegraphed to Garibaldi, that he could do nothing before the ministry was formed. The captain of the *Pharamond*, bitten by the bug of impatience too, sailed that night, leaving behind Garibaldi and his private army. Rations had to be issued to them.

Early next morning a telegram was sent to Florence asking for the decision. Florence's reply was to ask to be left in peace while the new ministry thought matters over. On the heel of that telegram came a new telegram to the harassed co-governor of Leghorn telling him he had done well to entertain the esteemed courageous Italian, but no decision could be taken yet. While the telegrams were flying Garibaldi did not remain idle. Regular troops broke barracks to fraternize with his men, Garibaldi showed himself in the theatre where he received a great ovation, windows were broken and as a result of all the commotion another telegram was sent to Florence asking Florence to take a decision, or to say at least whether the ministry wanted him there.

The new minister of war, d'Ayala, had six generals, and declared that, frankly, he needed no more. Garibaldi's impatience grew and his mood did not improve. "He begins to grumble," Florence was told. On 1st November the ministry capitulated. "Concede all that Garibaldi requires." The governors of Leghorn certainly sighed with relief when Garibaldi entrained for Florence.

Florence started to get rid of him as soon as he arrived.

It was quickly arranged that Garibaldi, having abandoned his attack on Sicily in the circumstances, would fight the Austrians instead, and therefore he should take his men to Ravenna. In Ravenna they would embark for Venice. To show their confidence in him they stipulated that he should surrender all arms, which would be returned at the point of embarkation. The people of Florence did not want the popular hero to go, yet go he did. He left Florence on 10th November with his army. He took his time, proceeding so slowly that General Latour was sent after him with a contingent of Swiss to egg him on. Garibaldi created no trouble, did not change his mind and his itinerary, and went to Ravenna as promised. The city council immediately begged him to move on.

Thus in less than six months after his return to Italy Garibaldi succeeded in making himself a perfect nuisance. He revelled in it, knew he was feared for it, knew too that it gave more power to his elbow, and appreciated that as a nuisance he could behave as he liked. In less than six months he had become a law unto himself. He had in a sense brought the outlook of the pampas to the soil of Italy. It was left to a far more subtle and intelligent man, namely to Count Cavour, to exploit to the full his nuisance value.

Garibaldi left Ravenna at the council's request. The idea was still to embark for Venice and to go to Manin's help. Nevertheless, he showed no desire any more for fighting in the last ditch for the Venetians. He remained with his men in the vicinity of Ravenna, and recruits flocked to him. They included some escaped convicts. Garibaldi did not mind them since he was of the opinion that if you fought for Italy then nothing else mattered. In memory of his legion of Montevideo he called his new private army the First Italian Legion.

They were a poorly equipped, poorly clad lot. They wandered through Umbria and the Marches, and to most of the inhabitants they seemed no better than bandits. Garibaldi was severe with the men and, his own sentiments notwithstanding, would punish them if they expressed with too much zeal their abhorrence of priests, monks and other enemies of the people. For some they were fine fellows spreading the democratic gospel: for others anarchist rabble. Though Garibaldi frowned on plundering he requisitioned food and whatever else he needed for his troops, consequently the *communes* were rather glad whenever the First Italian Legion decided to move elsewhere.

But the hour had already struck. On 15th November Count Pellegrino Rossi, the Papal minister, had been assassinated; on the 24th November the Pope had fled to Gaeta: all there was now left for Garibaldi to do was to enter Rome.

FROM ROME TO QUARTO

I

METTERNICH was right. Pio Nono's reforms and his liberalism brought about the revolution, and his position as a temporal ruler became analogous in the autumn of 1848 to that of Louis XVI's of France at the time of the king's attempt at escape. But whereas the king failed, the Pope made good his escape; and with that, liberalism as such ended for him. If he ever had a cat again it is pretty certain he would have dissuaded the cat from becoming a liberal. With the howling of the Roman mob still in his ear the Pope turned his back on Gioberti's ideas for good. From now on he would have no further truck with progress, as Montalembert and Monseigneur Dupanloup were to find out in time. In Gaeta, when thinking back on his reforms that followed the rigid rule of Gregory XVI, he probably remembered his predecessor's encyclical *Singulari Nos*:

> Lamentable is the spectacle presented by the aberrations of the human mind when it yields to the spirit of novelty; when acting contrary to the warning of the Apostle, it seeks to be more wise than it behoveth to be wise; and when relying too confidently on itself it thinks it can discover the truth outside the Church in which truth is found without the smallest shadow of error.

Pio Nono had yielded to the spirit of novelty, as a result of which he was at Gaeta, and lucky to have escaped with his life.

Pio Nono's attitude from now on could be best summed up in Mr E. E. Y. Hales's words in his excellent *Pio Nono*:[1]

> To Pio Nono the whole of the Papal State was part of the temporal patrimony of the Church, a patrimony with which she was invested by God to enable her to perform her spiritual function, a patrimony analogous to her religious buildings and all her other property, throughout the world, which went to make up the outward, visible, material part of her existence. It was sacrilegious to lay hand upon it in the same sense that it was sacrilegious to secularize a cathedral or to seize a monastery. He did not distinguish as his critics—particularly his Protestant critics—distinguished between one kind of Church property and another; nor, in reality, did he distinguish in the sense that they distinguished between his spiritual subjects and his temporal subjects. He always spoke of the "special character of Our sovereignty" even when he was speaking of his temporal power.

To that should be added his unshakable conviction that those who persecuted the temporal power wanted to annihilate the spiritual power too. There he was far from mistaken. Garibaldi, for instance, continued to hate the Church spiritual long after the temporal power ceased; in fact his hatred became even more intense when he saw that the Church survived the loss of the Papal State.

Today, with the wisdom distance gives, it is easy to consider Pio Nono stubborn and narrow-minded for not having seen that a free Church in a free state does no harm to the Church. But that he could not know, and his experiences in 1848 certainly did not persuade him that it would not damage the Church to lose the state. Those experiences made him fight even more stubbornly for the Patrimony of St Peter.

"Pio Nono has fled," wrote Mazzini to Aurelio Saffi,

[1] Eyre & Spottiswoode, London, 1954.

who was in Rome; "his flight is an abdication. An elective Prince leaves no dynasty behind him, you are therefore a Republic de facto because, except in the people, you have no source of authority. Once the people shall have formed a Government, the Italians, not yet free, would gather there, initiators and precursors of the future Italian Constituent."

Mazzini was not yet in Rome. His hopes were based on getting help from Guerrazzi, master of Tuscany at the time, and from Venice, which was still resisting, also from the French Republic. He could do nothing with Guerrazzi, whom he went to see in Florence. It was in Florence that he received a message of three words from Goffredo Mameli: "Rome, Republic, Come." Mazzini went. Garibaldi, however, had reached Rome long before him. When Mazzini appeared he was already a deputy, and was shouting "Viva la Repubblica!"

Before Mazzini's arrival, Rome, that is the Roman Republic, was governed by a triumvirate: Armellini, Saliceti and Montevecchi. After Mazzini's arrival a second triumvirate took over. The new triumvirate consisted of Mazzini, Armellini and Saffi, but it was Mazzini who was the ruling spirit. The Roman Republic meant for him putting, so to speak, God and the People into practice. For Garibaldi it meant fighting whomsoever was going to attack the cause he had espoused. Mazzini was the mind and the spirit, Garibaldi the sword, but the trouble often was that Garibaldi thought he had a mind too. Mazzini could not believe that France, the country of liberty, could turn against a sister republic; all Garibaldi saw was that the fight was on. If he irritated Mazzini with his lack of mind, Mazzini enraged Garibaldi because he tried to interfere with fighting matters about which, Garibaldi rightly thought, he himself knew infinitely more. Their antagonism was fundamentally as old as time: the man of action against the doctrinaire. For Garibaldi it was a war for an Italian republic, a war against tyranny: for Mazzini it was the birth of the Third Rome, the first Rome was the Rome of the Caesars, the second Rome of the Popes, and the third Rome of God and the People.

Mazzini was aware of the existence of the Catholic Powers who would not quietly stand by and let the Church be trampled on; he knew the French and appreciated that the Catholic Faith was deeply rooted in the Eldest Daughter of the Church even when she sported a Phrygian cap; such considerations were scorned by Garibaldi, who wanted to see the Sacra Bodega, that is the Holy Shop, closed, and denounced religious ceremonies "as useless symbols of a decrepit institution, which fostered in the people their tendencies to bigotry and superstition". Mazzini, on the other hand, wanted to prove before the world that his government did nothing to offend the feelings of Catholics. Garibaldi despised him for that in the same manner as he would despise Cavour for the French alliance. He may have learnt a lot while perusing the book of nature in his childhood, but where susceptibilities or finesse were concerned he remained completely illiterate.

Let it not be imagined that Garibaldi was received with much applause when he arrived in Rome and offered his sword to the first ministry. In the Papal State his and his legion's reputation proved disastrous. He who in the eyes of Piedmontese and Lombards was an admirable warrior, was looked upon at the beginning in Rome as a leader of bandits, a ferocious fellow who would burn and rob. (His faithful secretary and biographer Giuseppe Guerzoni is quoted here.) The government in Rome was not happy about his offer. As men of ideals they thought he was too dangerous. His friendship with Ciceruacchio, whose son murdered Rossi and who led the Trasteverino mob, did not endear him either with the government. They could not turn down the patriotic offer, besides he had men under arms, so they sought a way out, which they found by giving him the brevet of a lieutenant-colonel—Garibaldi had been known for years as General Garibaldi—and sent him to Macerata for the winter. They could not have made it more plain that they wanted to keep him out of Rome. Yet Garibaldi went off to Macerata without a murmur. There he took to drilling his men in earnest. If the government thought that he had come to seek position and power, then they were mistaken.

He kept away from Roman politics during the winter, spent his time acquiring arms and uniforms for his men, and was bristling for battle. It was soon to come. Meanwhile he started to make red shirts famous by ordering red shirts for every private in his legion. From now on wearing a red shirt meant that one was a Garibaldian; the red shirt meant too that one stood and fought for the Italian Revolution. Before the short-lived Roman Republic collapsed it had already become the custom to don a red shirt if one felt that one admired and believed in Garibaldi. It need hardly be mentioned that Mazzini never put one on.

Garibaldi loudly praised the foul murder of Count Rossi. In later years he would declare that any regicide was like a brother to him. But that was Garibaldi speaking. Garibaldi in action was innocent of sadism and cruelty. He committed no atrocities, refused to take part in assassinations, though such offers did come his way, and he never ill-treated an enemy who fell into his hands. However, that did not stop him from hobnobbing with assassins. When the time came for him to retreat from Rome he took with him Zambianchi, the murderer of Dominican and other

priests in the convent of San Calisto, and it was due to
Garibaldi that Zambianchi escaped with his life. Garibaldi
made him a member of The Thousand in 1860; and it is
interesting to relate because it throws light too on Garibaldi's relations with the second triumvirate, that when
Zambianchi went to London two years after his murders
he called on the triumvir Saffi, who turned the murderer
away from his door.

Garibaldi's first military action was to hold the road to
Naples at Rieti while Colonel Roselli went to put down
reactionary brigands. He arrived in Rieti at the end of
January 1849, and the inhabitants were in the beginning
more afraid of his legion than of the brigands. He admitted
that himself. After a time they came to like him, and he
rendered in the course of the winter signal service to the
republic by putting down reaction and brigandage, which
were, apparently, the same thing. On 5th February the
constituent assembly met in Rome, and it was Garibaldi,
seconded by Prince de Canino, who proposed that the
republic should be declared. He lustily shouted "Viva la
Repubblica!" It was remarked that if the fashionable word
had been monarchy, he would have shouted with equal
gusto "Viva la Monarchia!"

II

The fighting came in the spring. Catholic Europe did move,
including the French Republic, and Garibaldi went to
fight the Neapolitans, whom, anyway, it had been his
intention to fight before circumstances and events
outside his control brought him to Rome. Garibaldi was
made a general of division, but he was put under Roselli,
whom the triumvirs promoted to commander-in-chief.
Garibaldi was not the man to obey orders in military

matters. He believed he had learnt everything a military leader should know in South America; moreover, his instincts never failed him. Nobody, and certainly not Roselli, could change those ideas about himself, and they were not very wrong ideas either while his inordinate luck held out. The triumvirs thought that the quieter Roselli would damp Garibaldi's ardour. In that they were mistaken. Garibaldi led, and all Roselli succeeded in doing was to hamper his dash. Garibaldi's first victory was at Palestrina, but far more typical of the man and his luck was his next.

Roselli's plan of attack on the Neapolitans was to cross the Campagna towards Valmontone, then to take them in the flank. They found the Neapolitans in full retreat from the Alban Hills. Garibaldi, who had dashed ahead, saw that the withdrawing enemy might escape him. Disobeying his orders he decided to engage with the advance guard of King Ferdinand's army, and to ask Roselli to hasten the arrival of the central division. The point was that it was Garibaldi himself who was in charge of the central division, and not of the advance guard. Yet he gave orders to the advance guard, in fact put himself at their head. That was a perfect breach of discipline. The advance guard, however, was delighted to be led by him.

Forty of his lancers, after following the enemy, ran into a column of mounted men, the column turned on them and the lancers fled. When they came flying back Garibaldi became so furious that he reined up in their path. He sat there on his horse more immobile than many of his statues seem nowadays. The poor lancers tried in vain to pull up their horses, Garibaldi did not budge, and they all went down in a mass with Garibaldi at the bottom. The Neapolitan cavalry came charging towards the tangle of leader, men and horses. Some legionaries who were luckily nearby ran up, and the enemy was caught between two fires, was not only repulsed but left thirty prisoners behind; and the engagement was won by Garibaldi almost flattened out by the weight on him. He was so bruised that he could hardly move. His infantry now began to advance on the Neapolitans, driving them into Velletri, the central division coming up only afterwards. They came loudly cheering their undisciplined leader.

King Ferdinand, better known as King Bomba, continued his retreat towards Naples. It was probably while he lay under lancers and horses that Garibaldi took to despising the Neapolitan army. Though the king was in a hurry to withdraw in front of the enemy, the enemy commander-in-chief, Roselli, took no advantage of the situation, and let the Neapolitans slip out of Velletri. Garibaldi was convinced that he could have chased the Neapolitans as far as Naples and taken Naples as well. His march forward was stopped by Mazzini's orders at Rocca d'Arce, which was on the Neapolitan frontier. Garibaldi's comment was: "That Mazzini, who always had the mania of playing the general and did not understand it. . . ."

Even so staunch a latter-day Garibaldian as Dr G. M. Trevelyan disagrees with Garibaldi over the advance into Neapolitan territory, saying in his *Garibaldi's Defence of Rome*[1] that the general conditions of Italian politics were far less favourable for such an invasion than they would be in 1860; the tide was setting in the wrong direction and Italy was tired of revolution—"facts which Garibaldi, who was never tired, could not properly realize". That is logical enough, since a man who is always sure of himself and sees everything, history included, only through his own eyes can never be tired as long as he does not

[1] Longmans, Green & Co. 1928.

tire of himself, which Garibaldi was incapable even of imagining.

From his point of view the triumvirs' negotiations with Ferdinand de Lesseps are of no importance. Suffice to say that on 31st May de Lesseps signed an agreement with them, according to which the French were to protect the republic against all comers—de Lesseps, however, appended a clause according to which the treaty needed ratification by the French Republic; and that France never did, but sent vast reinforcements to the French general Oudinot, whose troops lay outside Rome and who gave notice to the Romans that the truce had ended. Now Garibaldi comes on the scene.

The triumvirs asked for his opinion on the crisis. The crisis had come about not by Oudinot receiving reinforcements but by the Roman Republic having been declared at all, or even, farther back, by the murder of Count Rossi and the flight of the Pope. Mazzini was deeply hurt; for it would have been different if the Neapolitans or the Austrians or the Spaniards had sent their forces against his Third Rome. Surely not the French Republic: yet the French Republic it was that came to bring it down and bring back the Pope. Garibaldi's considered opinion was that Garibaldi should be declared dictator of Rome with all the power that went with that word. He had a poor opinion of councils, ministries and assemblies.

The answer was no; in fact Roselli remained his commander-in-chief. Garibaldi did not feel hurt about that. He had told Mazzini that he could serve the republic only as dictator or as a simple soldier and asked him to choose. After Mazzini's refusal to make him dictator he returned to soldiering with the same zeal he would have displayed as dictator.

The defence of Rome was pretty hopeless for the Roman

Republic. The Roman army consisted at the utmost of eighteen thousand men, the great majority of whom had seen no fighting before. The French had forty-five battalions of infantry, eight squadrons of cavalry, seventy-six field guns and seventy siege guns. The Romans had about a hundred pieces all told. Mazzini still went on hoping, though his hopes were not based on being able to hold out indefinitely, but on France; and when the change came in Paris from constituent to legislative assembly he thought that the French attitude would become more friendly, or rather less inimical, to the triumvirate. It did not. So all there was left for him to hope in the flaming month of June 1849 was that the fall of his republic of God and the People would be as much a symbol and encouragement for Italians as their martyrs. Meanwhile Roselli, the commander-in-chief, and Garibaldi, his subordinate, continued to have unedifying rows.

The French attacked Rome. On Sunday, 3rd June, a French column under General Mollière came through the darkness before dawn south of the Pamfili enclosure, and blew a breach in the boundary wall. Another division appeared from the west, and found a gate of the Park left open. About four hundred Italians defended the Pamfili, but were taken by surprise and overpowered; half of them were captured, the other half made good their escape, reaching the convent of San Pancrazio and the Villa Corsini. The French who had entered through the open gate fell back on the Pamfili, then, joining up with Mollière's brigade, stormed the Villa Corsini, drove back the Italians and took the villa, which was the country house of the Corsini. It was almost like a fortress, built of massive stone, four stories high, dominating the neighbourhood, for which it was known as the House of the Four Winds. The two lower stories had no windows on the side facing Rome, an outside staircase led to the balcony on the second floor. That staircase would have to be mounted by any attacker. The grounds were full of trees, bushes and statues, and from the foot of the stairs ran a two-feet-high wall in both directions; on the wall stood large pots with orange trees in them giving cover to troops—now the French—holding the villa. The ground sloped towards Rome, bordered by a box hedge six feet high, and there was only one garden gate through which the villa could be stormed. In short, a hard nut to crack.

Garibaldi and his aide Masina were lodged at 59 Via delle Carozze near the Piazza di Spagna. Garibaldi was feeling ill, nevertheless he jumped out of bed when he heard the firing. He rushed to summon his troops, and had them assembled in front of St Peter's. He appreciated that if he tried to enter the Pamfili the French could push him back to the Vascello: so he started for the Janiculum by way of San Pietro in Montorio. The Legion left St Peter's at 5 a.m. and reached the Porta San Pancrazio at 5.30, Garibaldi wearing a white mantle and mounted on a white horse.

The French were in the Villa Corsini, which was four hundred yards away, with the ground rising high. The Italians were holding the Vascello. Garibaldi reined in his horse on an open space behind the Villa Corsini. He did not or with his military experience could not appreciate the strategical situation. His fighting experience was in open country; his eye was an eagle's when it surveyed the practically endless pampas; and he was a guerrillero, that is he needed room and space to attack, to vanish and to come back. He had neither on that 3rd June. His admirers put his strange strategy down to momentary ill-health, his detractors considered his behaviour frankly criminal, but

if one weighs up the odds one is bound to reach the conclusion that the sort of strategy the situation shrieked out
for was simply beyond his capacity and experience.

He started with sending one formation after the other
against the Villa Corsini. Each formation rushed through
the garden gate, then up the slope while deadly fire poured
on the advancing officers and men from every window.
If enough were left to reach the villa, they bayoneted
their way up that outside staircase, and held the drawing-
room till driven back by the French a few minutes
later. It is true that Garibaldi had hardly three thousand
men, but even his adulators admit that he sent them in
in too-small sections, thus making it doubly easy for the
French.

Courage, of course, did not desert him. There he sat
imperturbable on his white horse with bullets falling all
round him. Daverio, his chief of staff, was killed at his
side. Masina was already wounded, so was Nino Bixio,
the young man who had called on Charles Albert in 1847
to attack the Austrians and he would follow him. With
his tactics Garibaldi depleted his legion, and the legion was
now held together only by Garibaldi's magic. The white
mantle was riddled with bullet holes.

Manara's Bersaglieri came on the scene, and without
bothering to give them artillery support he threw them
against the villa. Led by Manara, Enrico Dandolo and
Hoffstetter the Swiss, the Bersaglieri, about three hundred
strong, charged the gate, then reaching the grounds they
were compelled to stop under withering French fire. Yet
the Bersaglieri did not retreat: they knelt down and
opened fire on the French. Enrico Dandolo was shot dead.
When at last the Bersaglieri started back after Manara
sounded the retreat, the real mowing down began; or as
Hoffstetter put it: ". . . the deadly harvest began in

earnest". When the survivors got back, Garibaldi at last ordered the guns on the walls of Rome to bombard the villa.

Now Garibaldi, who had witnessed the deadly harvest, did something that amounted to sheer idiocy. He went to find Emilio, the brother of the dead Enrico Dandolo, who was in charge of the Bersaglieri reserve. When he found him he ordered him to take twenty of his bravest men and charge the Villa Corsini at the point of the bayonet. He gave that order after the entire Legion and two companies of Bersaglieri had failed. One cannot help thinking that Garibaldi was under the impression that to dislodge the French regular army would be similar to attacking some band of Rosas that had crossed the River Paraná. If he thought that, he was soon disillusioned.

He enjoined on Emilio Dandolo to spare his ammunition and to use the bayonet at once. Eight men were killed as the brave little party advanced through the garden, French bullets halted them, and when they retreated only six of them were left. Emilio was among the wounded. When he came limping back he went to the Casa Giacometti where he found his brother's corpse.

At last, Garibaldi began to bombard the villa heavily. In the afternoon the French fire slackened, and taking advantage of it he sent Masina with forty lancers against the fortress-like villa. They galloped up the steps of the Corsini. Masina was killed. Infantry came behind, and once more they reached the villa. This time the French were pushed out of it, but only to retake it at the end of the day. At dusk the Bersaglieri were driven out of the Villa Valentini, and to Garibaldi were left only the Vascello and the Casa Giacometti. It was a complete defeat costing a thousand lives. (The Garibaldians tried to minimize the losses, putting them at five hundred men and fifty officers.)

The French losses were two hundred and fifty men and fourteen officers.

Yet it did no harm to the legend. The soldiers continued to love him, trust him and follow him, and in time the blame was put at Roselli's feet. He had thirteen thousand men with whom he was kept busy defending the Porta del Popolo, Porta San Giovanni, Ponte Molle and Monte Mario. Yet it was all his fault, said the Garibaldians, for not coming to Garibaldi's rescue.

III

Mazzini, pale and gentle, saw the corpses of the martyrs piling up. Nevertheless he was more determined to resist than the military leaders. He did not want to surrender; for surrender had no honoured place in his dreams. He lived within them, closing his eyes on the events that had already taken place. The catastrophe of Novara occurred on 22nd March. Meanwhile the Austrians were at Bologna. The Roman Republic was isolated in every sense. On 10th June Garibaldi failed again. He attacked the Villa Pamfili, but owing to sudden panic among his forces he had to retreat behind the walls. On the 12th, General Oudinot demanded surrender, which was refused. Now Garibaldi planned sorties which Roselli stopped because he said they were contrary to military rules. The French erected new batteries with which they bombarded the city. Everything began to happen as quickly as it happens when the end is in sight.

On 21st–22nd June the general French attack began. Garibaldi's headquarters were in the Corsini Palace inside the walls. There Mazzini, Roselli and Avezzana came to see him suggesting to him that he should put himself at the head of all troops and undertake to win back what had already been lost for good. Garibaldi refused. He by then considered further effort as useless butchery, and said he did not want to sacrifice "youths whom he loved as if they were his sons". Mazzini saw in his refusal proof of his belief that the republic was doomed. On 22nd June Sterbini proposed to Garibaldi that he should take over as dictator. Something of a full circle. Garibaldi, however, refused, and refused too to attack, which caused another row with Mazzini and Roselli. Sterbini rode through Rome shouting that Garibaldi should be made dictator. Garibaldi's mind was made up. He would fight till the end because it was his duty, but because the cause was lost he would do nothing else.

When the big artillery duel between attacker and defender started on the 22nd June even a child would have known that all was up. Yet on 30th June Rome was still holding out. Mazzini now dreamed of Rome being the last of the spirit of '48 to collapse. Garibaldi was at the Villa Spada hoping to hold back or delay the French at the bridge of Sant'Angelo. He was suddenly summoned to the assembly. He rode to it as fast as his horse could carry him, for he did not want to stay away from his troops too long. In the assembly three plans were to be debated. Surrender, fight till death, or to leave for the mountains taking along the government and the army. Garibaldi was all for the third plan. He declared he wished to take only volunteers with him. Surely the last thing that he wanted was to be straddled and riddled with doctrinaires and superiors. Mazzini supported him, and then Mazzini became angry because the assembly did not want to make obligatory the martial exodus from Rome. Against his protest the assembly passed this resolution:

In the name of God and the People:
This Constituent Assembly of Rome ceases from a defence that has become impossible and remains at its post.

Mazzini and the other triumvirs resigned, and, in a sense, Garibaldi was liberated. He was not at his best as a subordinate, he had no patience with dreamers; moreover, Rome had been like a strait-jacket for him. From now on he would obey only himself, would be free to move and take his own decisions. On 3rd July he assembled his troops and addressed them thus:

"Soldiers! That which I have to offer you is this: hunger, thirst, cold, heat; no pay, no barracks, no rations, but frequent alarms, forced marches, charges at the point of bayonet. Whoever loves our country and glory may follow me."

At four o'clock on that afternoon the cross-keyed banner of St Peter floated from the Castle of Sant' Angelo; and an eminent English historian referred to that as the usurpation of the Pope beginning again, which shows how much revolution is appreciated when it takes place in another country, and against an authority that is not one's own.

Five thousand men or so answered Garibaldi's call. It was a motley crowd, which included Zambianchi the murderer, Ciceruacchio and his two sons who were not averse to murder either, and Ugo Bassi the renegade priest. And there with him was Anita; for she had come to Rome and was at the Villa Spada during the last days. She had come like a tempest passing through enemy lines, pregnant though she was, arriving in Rome on 23rd June. She left her children with his mother at Nice. He wanted her to go back to them but she remained adamant. Garibaldi took from the defunct republic's treasury some money for his soldiers' immediate needs; he sold his watch for his own.

Garibaldi's plan was to get to Venice where Manin still resisted. Mazzini went to Civitavecchia where he boarded a steamer disguised as a steward. The steamer took him to Marseilles, from Marseilles he returned to London. Garibaldi and his followers left Rome in the darkness through the gate of San Giovanni, and soon he changed his mind. Rumour had it that Tuscany was waiting to rise and start another national revolution. So into Tuscany he would lead his men. General Oudinot calculated that Garibaldi would take to the hills of Albano and Frascati, therefore he occupied the two towns, and sent General Morris with his cavalry in pursuit of him. The Neapolitans were afraid that Garibaldi might invade the kingdom: Neapolitan troops occupied the Abruzzi. The Austrians occupied Umbria and the Marches, and sent mobile columns to intercept him at the Tuscan border. Garibaldi reached Terni on 9th July with his troops, then moved on to Tivoli, Monticelli, Monte Rodondo, Poggio Mirtillo, then entered the Apennines. He was in his element.

When he reached Arezzo he found the gates closed to him, and at Montepulciano he was shot at. Tuscany, evidently, did not want him. He reverted to his original plan of going to Venice. On the 13th they reached Lodi with only three thousand followers left. The rest had deserted, and desertions continued, reducing his ranks daily. General d'Aspre in Florence and another Austrian general, Gorkowski, in Bologna sent out troops to find him. The French did the same from Viterbo. Garibaldi had but fifteen hundred men left at the end of July when he reached the tiny Republic of San Marino. He sent his quartermaster to the authorities asking for safe passage and food for his troops. The authorities were not keen to accede to his request since the Austrians were not far away, nevertheless they promised to let him and his men have food provided they stayed outside the boundary.

Garibaldi sent Ugo Bassi into San Marino. Night had already set in. He was given supper by a patriot, and

looking out through the window after supper he saw the
bivouac fires of the Austrians. He had an urgent message
delivered to Garibaldi, who now had only one alternative
left to being surrounded and cut down by the Austrians,
namely to throw himself on the mercy of the little republic.
At dawn on 31st July he marched his men up into San
Marino, where he was received in the Hall of Audience
by the Citizen-Regent, and the Captains of the Republic.
"All hail to the fugitives," they said, "as such we will
receive you."

The red shirts were in rags, many of the followers could
hardly hold themselves up any longer; there were women
too among them, and old men, and boys not older than
fourteen. When they had eaten the food the good people
of San Marino provided for them, Garibaldi posted on the
church door his last Order of the Day.

"Soldiers," it said, "we have arrived in a land of refuge.
We must maintain an irreproachable conduct towards our
generous hosts, since it will gain for us the respect merited
by our misfortunes. From the present moment I release all
my companions in arms from every engagement, leaving
them free to re-enter private life. But I would remind you
that it is better to die than to live as slaves to a foreigner."

Many of the poor companions in arms sold what was
left of their equipment so as to be able to go home. A
touching episode was the case of the little cannon, which
was the only cannon the Garibaldians had left. While he
was still in the Hall of Audience some of his men tried to
push it up to San Marino. The Austrians fired on them;
most of them fled up Monte Titano, but Anita immediately urged her horse to the cannon, shouting:
"Where is Peppino?" Peppino came galloping down the
road and steadied the men as much as was possible; the
little cannon, however, stayed behind.

The Austrian commander-in-chief, the Archduke Ernest, whom the Citizen-Regent had gone to see to intercede for Garibaldi and his men, refused naturally enough to let Garibaldi go; after long negotiations he agreed, however, to Garibaldi going free on the condition that he took himself to America. The archduke's terms were considered too severe both by Garibaldi, who in the end did go to America, and by the host of his biographers. In fact, if one considers what an unpleasant thorn he was in Austria's side, the condition was comparatively generous, and would certainly not have been the same a century after.

Garibaldi decided to escape, and to get to Venice. He begged Anita to stay behind in San Marino. Her answer was: "You want to leave me." That in her language meant that she would follow him. He confided his plan only to a few, who included Ciceruacchio and Bassi. They vanished in the night, and between midnight and dawn they got through the Austrian lines. He left behind a note saying: "The conditions imposed on me by the Austrians I cannot accept, and therefore we cease to encumber your territory." When his men learnt in the morning that he had gone, dismay was general. The San Marino authorities gave each a passport for Rimini and two *paoli*. That was the end of the army Garibaldi had offered hunger, thirst, cold, heat, no pay and no rations. They had the lot.

Garibaldi, Anita and their companions reached Cesenatico on the Adriatic. Anita was very ill by then. It was the night of 1st August. She had high fever, nevertheless embarked with the rest in the thirteen fishing boats which some fishermen lent them, and they set sail for the mouth of the Po. The Austrian fleet was not idle, and only four of the fishing boats reached port. In one boat were Garibaldi and Anita. "I took," he was to relate, "my precious wife in my arms, disembarked, then deposited her

Garibaldi in his prime

(*Photograph by Alinari*)

The last portrait of Anita Garibaldi,
Garibaldi's first wife

Underneath it is written: "This
photograph was taken from a
miniature commissioned by Garibaldi and left to their daughter
Teresita." The photograph is
now in the possession of Museo
del Risorgimento Italiano

on the shore." That was at Mesoli. He then carried her into a cornfield, where she lay resting her head on his knee with only one of his comrades keeping them company. Then they went to the house of a peasant and changed their clothes. Meanwhile the Austrians, infuriated by Garibaldi's escape from San Marino, were scouring the countryside. General Gorkowski, who commanded them, issued a proclamation in which he threatened with death all who would help the fugitives in any manner. Garibaldi was referred to as a chief of bandits and criminals, and Anita was described as a woman six months gone with child.

They eventually found asylum on the Guiccioli farm, which stood in the middle of the pine forest of Ravenna. Garibaldi put Anita on a little bed, and, dead tired, he lay down to sleep. A doctor had already come and gone. When he saw Anita he exclaimed: "But you called me to a corpse." When Garibaldi woke up she asked for water. He held a glass to her lips, she drank a little, then died. A minute later a man rushed into the room crying the Austrians had surrounded the farm. Garibaldi first dug her a grave, and only then escaped. That is one version.

According to another version, Mme Schwartz's, and she claims it as "the most authentic truth", the Austrians surrounded the farm while Garibaldi slept, and it was only by a miracle that Garibaldi was able to escape through one door while his pursuers were entering by another. It was at that very moment that Anita must have died. "Then either to save the corpse of the unfortunate woman, warm as it was," she continues, "from the brutal soldiery, or to remove from his house this too convincing proof of Garibaldi's presence, the farmer buried the body of the heroic Brazilian in the sandy soil of the forest but with such

inconsiderate haste that when his panic of fear was dis-
sipated no one could tell where she was laid." Mme
Schwartz goes on to relate that some months after the
flight of Garibaldi through the Pineta a farm labourer
thought that he saw a wild boar turning up the soil a little
way from the house, and examining the spot carefully "he
assured himself that the animal, having already devoured
the right hand of the unfortunate Anita, who had not been
buried deep enough in the ground, was preparing to
disinter the entire body".

Guerzoni, however, tells us that a fortnight after Anita's
death some peasants saw a hand sticking out of a sand-hill.
They called the authorities, the body was exhumed, and
they found that it was the partially decomposed body of a
woman with her tongue sticking out, the windpipe
broken, a conspicuous red circle round the neck, and a
six-month-old foetus in her entrails. An autopsy was
carried out by the Pontifical authorities, and it was
established that the woman's death was caused by strangu-
lation. The news spread through the Romagna, but Guerzoni was of the opinion that Anita's death was caused by a
haemorrhage that choked her. After the autopsy she was
re-interred.

Garibaldi visited her tomb in September 1859 with
Mme Schwartz, and, writes Mme Schwartz, "the coffin
with the ashes of the brave Anita was soon transported to
Nice. Wishing to see a monument raised to the Brazilian
heroine, I opened a subscription for this purpose in Garibaldi's native town. But this subscription unfortunately
came to nothing, and the last time I visited Nice I found
that Anita's remains had been buried on the Castle Hill,
and there was nothing to indicate the particular spot."

Anita was in life an almost more intransigent atheist
than her husband. When she had visited him in Rieti and

the two of them rode out they met a procession. It was Good Friday. In order to please the population, or perhaps in order not to enrage it, Garibaldi dismounted and doffed his hat; Anita remained seated on her horse. After her death Garibaldi canonized her in his private paradise, where, one hopes for her sake, she met kindred spirits, such as the Chevalier de la Barre.

Her death added to Garibaldi's stature. She was the hero's martyr wife, the deeply loved spouse, who, they were to say in time, died for Italy; and this writer saw in his boyhood a coloured print showing Anita being shot dead by the Austrians in pitched battle. She was on horseback and wore a red shirt. Naturally Garibaldi was at her side.

Ciceruacchio and Bassi were condemned to death at Bologna and executed on 8th August.

Garibaldi, after escaping from the farmhouse in which lay his dead or dying wife, managed to gain the outskirts of Forli. Luckily for him, but lucky he was, the gate of the town, which usually was closed at night, had been left open because of a big fire in a barn full of straw. The town was in turmoil, thus Garibaldi and his only companion, Leggiero, managed to reach Dr Zattini's house unobserved. On the night of 21st August they were conducted to Modigliana, where a priest called Giovanni Verita, but known as Don Zuan, awaited the fugitives. They would, Don Zuan explained, have to cross the torrential Tramezzo. He explained too that the Tramezzo was dangerous, therefore he would wade across, carrying them one after the other on his shoulder.

"I know water," observed Garibaldi.

"You know the sea but not our torrents," replied Don Zuan, who then carried Leggiero across the Tramezzo. On his return he told Garibaldi to get on his shoulder. "Are we perhaps on the bank of the Rio Grande, or the Niagara, or the Tevere?" asked Garibaldi sarcastically.

"This river has no importance, but it's a traitor," said Don Zuan. Garibaldi gave him a long scrutinizing look. He saw the priest was not joking, so let himself be carried across the torrent.

From Ravenna Garibaldi wrote to a friend in Florence inquiring whether there was any chance of starting a revolution in Tuscany. Garibaldi had already given up all thought of pushing on to Venice, where resistance was coming to an end. Without red shirts, doctrines and the noise of bravado Manin held out till 24th August, then negotiated an honourable capitulation. No quarrels, no reproaches and no controversies followed him into exile. He died in Paris in 1857, and well deserved the public funeral the Venetians gave him when his remains were brought back to the town for which he fought so nobly.

The Tuscan friend suggested to Garibaldi an itinerary through Tuscany in lieu of a revolution. Garibaldi followed the itinerary in the company of Leggiero. He passed through the country full of Austrian troops. One day while he sat outside an inn some Austrians spoke to him, asking him whether he had seen the Red Devil anywhere. While he answered their questions skilfully, he held his hands before his face, so the Austrians could not see it, and thus he avoided recognition. They must have been very simple Austrians.

He and Leggiero reached Spezzia; from there they drove in a carriage to Chiavari, where the commandant begged Garibaldi not to start disturbances. His nuisance value had preceded him. The commandant had them escorted to Genoa, where they were received with all respect due to them by King Victor Emmanuel's general La Marmora, and put politely behind bars. The general informed the government of Turin of the arrival and detention of his honoured guest. It was decided that he should be kept in custody, but was allowed out on parole to visit his family in Nice. There he saw his mother and his children, returned to Genoa, and shortly after he was set at liberty on the condition that he left Italy, which he did, and with that the second exile began.

IV

It is unlikely that Garibaldi troubled to weigh up the events in Italy and his part in them between his return from the first exile and his setting out on the second. He had certainly been a flaming sword in that period. He had skirmished with the Austrians, had twice defeated the Neapolitans; but the French beat him. That would remain unchanged even in the future; for he would skirmish with the Austrians again, would defeat the Neapolitans again, and at his next encounter with the French, at Mentana in 1867, the French would thrash him again.

The battles of Palestrina and Velletri had turned him more into the Italian military hero than even the legend demanded; Rome had not been a success, whichever way one looks at it, yet it added to his fame in spite of 3rd June, and in spite of him having lost so many of those youths whom he loved like a father. The retreat to San Marino was something he alone could have achieved, and now that he was leaving Italy he left in Italy his own courage, as it were, for the Italians to feed on.

In his exile he chose his old friend the sea. Not for him the gas-lit cosiness of the exiles' life in London, with all the chatting, whispering, quarrelling and plotting that went with it. He would not have cared to spend his time with Mazzini, Kossuth, Ledru-Rollin, Louis Blanc, and the others, and would not have cared a damn for their dreams, rows, manifestoes and the rest of the exiles' bag of tricks. He would have found the gas-lit life desolate and meaningless. Let Holyoake try out bombs intended for the French emperor by Felice Orsini (Orsini and Mazzini quarrelled in time, of course) in the peaceful English countryside; let Mazzini and Kossuth say the same things while meaning something different; and let the other pillars of the Roman Republic recriminate while a ship rolled under him on the other side of the world. Besides, the revolutionaries did not really consider him as one of them, and when he became the Sardinian king's champion, in their eyes he let the sacred cause down. Yet Garibaldi could rightly have told them that it was he, who feared not death and whose sword had remained unsheathed during the whole bloody month of June, who was the one who saved Rome from complete carnage when the dreamers insisted on it.

So he returned to the sea, which sets him so completely apart from the plotters and schemers of his time. He first wanted to go to Tunis, but the French government let the Bey of Tunis know that France would not be pleased if Garibaldi were given asylum. He was forbidden to land in any of the Barbary ports. He sailed for Malta, where he was not well received, in fact was told to disembark instead on the island of La Maddalena. There he was well received by the mayor, and he spent quiet days hunting and fishing; and gazing out to sea he beheld the isle of Caprera, with which he fell in love. At the beginning of the New Year of 1850 the Sardinian ship of the line, the *Colombo*, cast anchor outside La Maddalena with orders to take Garibaldi to Gibraltar. It had, after all, been arranged that he should leave Sardinian territory. Garibaldi complied with the order, embarked in the *Colombo*, and was shipped to Gibraltar, where the governor permitted him to land only for twenty-four hours, and he was carefully watched till he left for Tangier. The Sardinian consul in Tangier received him with open arms, and while staying with him Garibaldi started to write his memoirs, out of which grew Dumas's book, and another by Elpis Melena (Mme Schwartz). Although Garibaldi was a master of stirring clichés and rabble-rousing right words, he was but a poor performer with the pen, as we shall see when we reach his novels.

He inquired from the Spanish consul whether Spain would give him asylum: as if Spain had not enough of her own soldiers to disturb her peace. The consul's reply was a crisp no. Turkey was the only European country left that might perhaps take him in. In the end the American consul came to the rescue, offering him a free passage to America, which Garibaldi accepted, sailed for Liverpool, from which port he left for America. He thus carried out the Archduke Ernest's wish.

In New York there were plenty of Italians and other admirers to rally round him and help him. Kossuth at the time was in full limelight in the United States, cheered and fêted wherever he went. Garibaldi was not interested in that kind of fame, and many Americans could not appreciate that the swashbuckler was also a retiring person, and was criminally uninterested in coining money. He went to work for a tallow-chandler, and all he got, it seems, out of his job were three huge candles his employers sent to him on Caprera long after he left America. One candle was red, the second white and the third green, and they were accompanied with a note that optimistically said: "A present to General Garibaldi, to make a tricoloured illumination with on the Campidoglio when he gets to Rome." That was not to be.

Of his tallow-making period his one comment was, as

he looked back on New York, that tallow-making made
him sick, and he could never master the art. He kept away
from other exiles such as Ledru-Rollin, Louis Blanc,
Lamartine and Felix Pyat, who were in no better situation
than he; and he went back to sea. He visited South
America again, entered into the service of Don Pedro de
Negro in Lima, and captained a trading ship between
Peru and Hong Kong. After a time he returned to New
York, and was appointed the skipper of a small vessel,
the *Commonwealth*, which sailed under the American flag,
but was owned by an Italian, and most of the crew were
Italian too. She put into Newcastle-upon-Tyne on one of
her voyages.

Meanwhile Mazzini did not remain idle in London.
With Aurelio Saffi, Picozzi and Piolti he planned another
plot with ponderous deliberation. A rising was to take
place in Milan. As there were eighteen Austrian sentries
at the main gate of the citadel, eighteen patriots were
instructed to assassinate them. It should be done precisely
at 5 p.m. because Radetzky and his staff would be dining
at that hour. A hundred other patriots were to murder
them. The populace should be roused simultaneously in
the streets and all Austrian officers who were walking in
the streets were to be murdered too. Mazzini appeared on
the Swiss–Italian frontier and gave the signal for 6th
February 1854. The plot failed miserably. Some two
hundred conspirators turned up, but it was over in an
hour. The balance was ten Austrians killed and wounded,
sixteen patriots executed, and a hundred condemned to
prison in the fortresses of Austria. The Hungarian troops
were sent back to Austria. The reason is of some interest
since it sheds light on a world with which Garibaldi would
have nothing to do. (He had learnt his lesson on the day he
waited in vain in Genoa for the conspirators to turn up.)

It had been arranged, still in London, between Mazzini and that polyglot giant Kossuth that, in Mazzini's words, "when Louis Kossuth was about to make a journey of indefinite duration through the United States of America, it was agreed upon between us that he should sign and leave with me a proclamation to the Hungarian regiments serving in Italy, calling upon them to support any national movement that might take place there, and that I should sign and give to him a proclamation to the Italian regiments serving in Hungary for the same purpose. And we did this . . . each of us therefore was to have full authority to affix a date to the proclamation in his hands, and to make use of it when he should think fit. . . . The first news of the insurrection that reached London brought no details, and Kossuth was so roused that he applied to my friend Stansfield for pecuniary aid in order to join me, which was given. But when the news of our defeat arrived next day Kossuth . . . hastened to declare through the English press that the proclamation to the Hungarians was purely and simply an invention of my own. . . ."

Mazzini wrote a letter to the *Daily News* saying that the original proclamation signed by Kossuth was still in his hands, and anybody who was interested could look at it. "This," said Mazzini, "was enough for the English public." When Mazzini returned from Switzerland Kossuth calmly went to see him and "embraced me with the air of one deeply moved, and uttered not a syllable with regard to the proclamation". Mazzini shrugged his shoulders and kept his peace. Kossuth would not have done so well with Garibaldi in similar circumstances, nor would Garibaldi have held his peace.

It was a year after the ghastly Milanese attempt that the *Commonwealth* put into Newcastle. Garibaldi's fascination for the English was profound, and his having fought against the Pope especially endeared him to the vast majority of the nation. Newcastle gave him a rousing welcome, and Joseph Cowan presented him in the name of the citizens with a telescope and a gold-hilted sword. A deputation waited on him at Shields where his ship lay, and he said modestly: "I am very weak in the English language and I can but imperfectly express my acknowledgment of your great kindness." They found his modesty admirable, and they took him even more to their hearts when in a letter to John Cowan he wrote: "If England at any time in a just cause may need my arm, I am ready to unsheath in her defence this noble and splendid sword, received at your hands." On the sword were engraved these words: "To General Garibaldi from the People of Tyneside, friends of European Freedom." On top of it all his English admirers proposed a toast on board the *Commonwealth*: "Mazzini, the illustrious compatriot of Garibaldi." One can almost see through the mist of a century Garibaldi necking his glass down, but, alas, one cannot see the look in his eyes.

Garibaldi handed over the *Commonwealth* to an American captain, then took rail to London. He remained there for a while, saw Mazzini now and then, and a rich English widow fell in love with him. He became engaged to her, the engagement lasting for two years. But before continuing with the widow, Jessie White had better be introduced. She was born in 1832 at Gosport, the daughter of a well-known yacht builder. Educated at several private schools, she became a freethinker, and drank in the teachings of the heretical preacher George Dawson. She finished her education in 1851 and began to teach and write. She published a book called *Alice Lane* about humble life in Yorkshire. She was an admirer of Lamennais, and wrote an article on him in the *Biographical Magazine*; and she became Mazzini's humble disciple. For her, Mazzini could do no wrong; he was in her eyes perfect in every sense; in her heroes' gallery he was the tops. Garibaldi came second, and when one reads her partisan, though excellent, *The Birth of Modern Italy*,[1] which is in fact her collected posthumous papers by the Duke Litta-Visconti-Arese, it is fascinating to watch her seriously persuading herself, if not the reader, that Mazzini and Garibaldi loved each other dearly and saw eye to eye.

Jessie White did not only love her heroes: in the course of Garibaldi's dash through Sicily and the Neapolitan Kingdom, and especially at the battle of the Volturno, she nursed his sick soldiers under enemy fire. In 1857 she married Alberto Mario. She went with Garibaldi to Dijon in 1870, and nursed his soldiers there too. She died poor and forgotten in 1906 as a teacher at the Provincial Normal School in Florence. Her husband predeceased her. Rightly Carducci said of her that she was a great woman to whom Italians owed a huge debt.

Now Jessie White was a friend of the rich widow in 1854, and all one gets out of her is that "it would have been fortunate for him [Garibaldi] and his children if his scruples, when he ascertained the extent of her fortune and the disdainful attitude assumed by her eldest son, had not decided him to give her back her freedom and retain his own". One somehow understands the eldest son. It must have seemed a pretty grim prospect to a young Victorian gentleman to envisage Garibaldi as a prospective stepfather. Garibaldi himself summed up his own appearance around that time when the painter Daniel Felton, who did his portrait, still in New York, for an Italian enthusiast, remarked that Garibaldi had a likeness to Christ, but with the wisdom of the serpent in his eye. "The Christ type as

---

[1] T. Fisher Unwin, London, 1909.

you call it," remarked Garibaldi, "is not uncommon on the Ligurian coast where I was born; and perhaps it may be accounted for by the wives of sailors in peril going to pray before pictures and images of Jesus. As for the serpent's wisdom, or wariness, that undoubtedly was induced by the danger in which the population, including my own ancestors, has stood for centuries past from Algerian pirates." Certainly not the picture of the ideal stepfather for a rich, young subject of the Queen.

Garibaldi was more forthcoming than Jessie White about the widow, whose name was Emma Roberts, and who had a fine house in London. He did not care for her worldly habits and way of life. "At every step a servant," poor Garibaldi cried, "and a set meal every three hours, and no fixed time for going to bed. A month of this sort of life would have killed me!" One sees Mrs Roberts drinking weak tea while Garibaldi longs for a fried thrush, with a drink of half wine, half water, to wash it down with. Still, they remained friends, called each other "tu", and it was said of her that she was his only woman who dared to speak to him frankly about his faults; but one fears she spoke more of table manners than of matters that were of more intrinsic importance to him.

He led a retiring life while he was in London. Mazzini, Jessie White relates, introduced him to his circle of friends; and when Garibaldi was leaving England the two men were still friends. As proof of that she quotes a note Mazzini sent to Mrs Nathan in which he asked her to be at Blackwall Station, Fenchurch Street, on the next day at 12.30 so that they should all go to greet Garibaldi together on his ship. Garibaldi took command of the *Commonwealth* again, and sailed her to Genoa. His friend-ship for Mazzini did not outlast the voyage.

V

The situation was now signally different in Italy; for the ball of liberation had passed into the hands of Piedmont, thanks to Victor Emmanuel and his great minister, Cavour. Cavour did not believe in *Italia farà da se*: he believed in finding allies who would help Italy to chase out the Austrians and unite her under the House of Savoy, which he faithfully served. Cavour was no friend of the revolution, in fact he feared it for the anarchy it might bring about. He despised the revolution at the same time because it had got Italy nowhere. Mazzini said of Cavour that he wanted the French alliance because he was afraid of the revolution, which, without any need for an alliance, would have freed Italy alone. Cavour feared the revolution, but only in the sense that it would bring about ruination; for he was convinced that the revolution would never do more for Italy than it had done already, or than the experience of thirty years of unsuccessful insurrections and ill-fated conspiracies had shown it capable of doing. How could the boast of *l'Italia farà da se* be realized by a small state like Piedmont with four million inhabitants, which could never collect sufficient troops against three hundred thousand tried troops that Austria could pour into Italy? He did not shrug off Novara and Custozza as so many of his fellow countrymen did. Moreover, Cavour believed in settled institutions, and he was intimately enough acquainted with the outside world to appreciate that the two sympathetic powers, England and France, would not help Italy if unification were to end in anarchy.

Firstly, it was important to forestall the revolution; secondly, allies had to be found, that is to say wooed. Forestalling the revolution meant to achieve the unification without the revolution taking a hand in it. Mazzini was the embodiment of the revolution, therefore whenever Cavour and the king, who looked like a small though proud and sturdy tomcat, took a decision, they invariably had to bear Mazzini in mind. He had immense power and influence in the affairs of state, albeit from a long distance; and king and minister, who had never spoken to him and who did not rescind his exile even after 1859, lived, as it were, continuously with him. Mazzini was the shadow that would turn into flesh and blood if they did not get on with achieving Italia Unita.

To find an ally was Cavour's second preoccupation: as a matter of fact it grew out of the first; and when the Crimean War started he had the happy thought of sending a Sardinian corps to the Crimea to fight at the side of England and France, the two countries he needed for his plans against Austria. The Sardinian contingent sailed for the Crimea under the command of General La Marmora. Cavour suffered true anguish till news came of the Sardinian victory at the battle of Tchernaya. The king, Cavour and the whole of Turin were jubilant. It appeared to them almost as though Custozza and Novara were revenged. It was a grave risk that Cavour took; for had the Italians not distinguished themselves at Tchernaya his clever idea would have but helped the revolution, apart from having done nothing to endear Italy with the two powers he was courting.

Cavour was a remarkable man, kind, astute, cunning, a grand seigneur, a faithful friend, and in politics utterly unscrupulous. A good example of his cunning was that even in death he indulged in some double-crossing to attain his end. Before his death he had made sure that a Franciscan friend of his, Fra Giacomo, would give him the last sacraments in spite of the Bull of Excommunication; and the last sacraments were given to him who had conceived the plan of invading Papal territory only a year before, and thanks to whom the Pope lost nearly all the Patrimony of St Peter. Yet it was the Pope who remarked to M. d'Ideville some years after Cavour's death that Cavour was a true Italian, and expressed his hope that God would forgive him as he, Pio Nono, had.

Cavour was born in the Via del Arcivescado in Turin, and there he lived till the end of his life. He fought a duel as a young man. Afterwards his adversary said he had heard the bullet whizz past his ears. "J'ai tiré pour vous manquer," was Cavour's answer. During a violent outbreak of cholera in Turin he visited the hospital daily. He was always generous to adversaries, and was the first to regret it when he lost his temper or fell out with a friend. It once happened that he lost his temper with Farini and Torelli, who were still comparatively unknown men. He wrote to them on the following day requesting them to see him on urgent business. They returned no answer. He asked them again—no reply. So things went on till one day Torelli, walking in Turin, felt an arm pass through his, and Cavour's voice whispering: "*Avete capito che non voglio bronci?*" (Haven't you understood that I don't want any grudges?)

He was squat, pot-bellied, had stumpy legs, short round arms with hands always in the trouser pockets, a thick neck in which you could see the veins swelling, scant thin hair, blurred blotched face, grey eyes and goggle spectacles. He usually wore a snuff-coloured tail-coat, grey creased trousers, black silk double tie, crumpled shirt, brown satin single-breasted waistcoat, half unbuttoned as if he needed breath, and a short massive gold chain dangled in front. The Pope, as we have seen, was to forgive him though he took most of his state from him: there was one man, however, who never forgave him but hated him vilely, malignantly for the rest of his life. That man was Garibaldi.

It did not start like that. In fact when Garibaldi arrived back in Italy he was, for instance, all on Cavour's side where the expedition to the Crimea was concerned. Naturally Mazzini was against it, though if it had failed he would have profited from it. Jessie White had reluctantly to admit that in the Crimean matter Garibaldi was right and her hero wrong, and speaking of Cavour she said: "At the helm of Piedmont, now just recovering from her calamities, Fortune had placed a man greater and more hard-headed than Bismarck, as unscrupulous as Metternich, and as high-handed as Palmerston."

She and Mrs Roberts went to Italy soon after Garibaldi's return, Mrs Roberts taking her daughter, but not her son. They met Garibaldi in Nice, and they travelled with him to Sardinia, where Garibaldi went boar-hunting with the local gentry. The ladies found that one month of Sardinia was plenty. They continued their journey to Rome, Garibaldi returned to Nice, and when the ladies joined him there on their return from Rome they found him delighted with the news of the arrival of the Piedmontese Expeditionary Corps at Balaclava, for Garibaldi was all for fighting and winning military laurels, whereas Jessie White's true hero was all for plotting and conspiracies.

The ladies travelled back to England in May 1855, taking with them Garibaldi's second son Ricciotti, who had a bad leg. He was cured by English specialists, then went to school for a time in England. In the following year Garibaldi came to England again, staying with Jessie White's father at Portsmouth and with her in London. He was a quiet man in those days, since there was no bugle-call, no neighing of chargers, and no glinting bayonets. He discussed Italian matters in an almost detached manner with his friend Jessie. "If a general rising of the people of Italy could be ensured, there would be no necessity to

Pope Pius IX at Velletri, eight miles from the Papal summer residence, Castel Gandolfo, on 11th March 1863
He is in one of the railway carriages built in Paris in 1858 and presented to him by the Rome-Civitavecchia Railway Company.

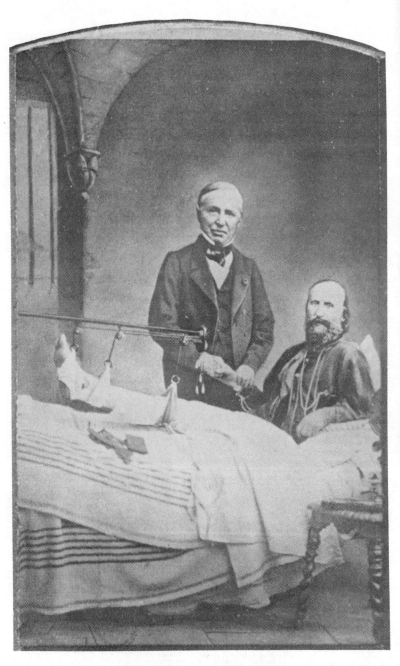

Garibaldi with his doctor after the
Battle of Aspromonte, 1862

wait for kings or diplomacy, but at this moment especially, no one will stir hand or foot: the bravery and patience under hardships of the Sardinian contingent in the Crimea has awakened the pride of our people. You know how unpopular the war was, how only the king and Cavour carried the day in teeth of the opposition. . . . Believe me, there could be no greater mistake than to choose this moment for a rising." Those were the words of a serious, much-travelled seafarer who had learnt wisdom from experience.

As a matter of fact he was thinking of a *coup de main* on the Neapolitan Kingdom with the object of liberating some of King Bomba's political prisoners. His brother Felice had died and left him a sum of money, which enabled him to buy part of that rock of an island: Caprera. In England he wanted to buy a cutter to ply to and fro between Genoa and Caprera while building his house on his rock. It was at Caprera that he wanted to reunite his family. The plot for the *coup de main* had been hatched by Sir William Temple, British Ambassador in Naples, Sir James Hudson, British Ambassador in Turin, Antonio Panizzi of the British Museum, and Dr Agostino Bertani, who would become a bad influence on Garibaldi during The Thousand, and who would become the leader of the extreme left in the Italian Parliament. Giacomo Medici came over to England, and bought a ship, the *Isle of Thanet*, which got wrecked off Yarmouth. That stopped the enterprise for a while. A new subscription was started for it, among the subscribers being Mrs Gladstone and Lord and Lady Holland, and Jessie White believed that Lord and Lady Palmerston subscribed too, anonymously. Eventually it all came to nothing because Sir William Temple thought he could get an amnesty for the prisoners on condition that they went to America. Sir William became ill, returned to England and died. The prisoners were amnestied in 1859, sent to America, liberated on the high sea by Luigi Settembrini, and then proceeded to England, where they were received enthusiastically because they were, Jessie White sadly remarks, "constitutionalists", which, of course, her hero Mazzini was not. (One should bear in mind that generally the English in their enthusiasm for the liberation of Italy, which could make two British ambassadors behave as unprofessionally as Hudson and Temple, preferred the patriots who wanted Italia Unita without the revolution, and rather disapproved of those who were for the revolution. That Garibaldi appreciated, and acted on it when in Sicily and Naples.)

Garibaldi saw Panizzi in London, but did not go near Mazzini. From London he returned to Portsmouth, and was "adored by every man, woman, and child in the house and shipyard, where he delighted the shipwrights by the knowledge he displayed of the smallest detail of their craft". Then Garibaldi went back to Caprera.

In 1856 more plots were afoot. There was a rising in Sicily, and its leader, Baron Francesco Bentivegna, was shot. At the end of the year, after Agesilao Milano's attempt to assassinate King Bomba failed owing to the mail-shirt the king wore, Carlo Pisacane and Roselino Pilo still believed that an attack on Sicily would prove successful if Garibaldi led it. They approached him, and his answer was no. Jessie White wrote to him asking the reason why he refused. Garibaldi wrote back to her in the loving manner he adopted when writing to women, which made some of them believe that they were confessions of love, and even offers of marriage.

"Sister beloved," he wrote, "whatever happens, I never meant to vex you, and should be grieved at heart if I have done so. You certainly have no need of tenderness, and I am far from wasting it on you; but what you cannot hinder me from saying is the truth. Well, I love you, which matters very little to you; I love you for myself and for my boy, and for Italy, which I idolize and venerate above all earthly things. . . ." He went on to assure his sister that he dared take rank with the most staunch of Italian patriots, but he was not the man to offer himself as chief of an attempt when he saw no possibility of success. Then he spoke of Piedmont. "In Piedmont there is an army of forty-five thousand men and an ambitious king; these are elements for an initiative, and for success, in which the majority of Italians believe today. Let your friend [Mazzini] furnish similar elements, and show a little more practicality than he has done hitherto, and we will bless him also and follow him with fervour. On the other hand, if Piedmont hesitates and proves itself unequal to the mission which we believe it is called upon to fulfil, we shall repudiate it. Let any one, in short, commence the Holy War with temerity even, and you will see your brother first on the battlefield. . . ."

That letter is practically a confession of his faith. He would fight for the Sardinian king with the same gusto as for the revolution if there were a chance to push out the foreigner. Since Cavour forestalled the revolution Garibaldi fought in 1859 for the king, which, of course, saddened the revolutionaries. For him it was the natural thing to do.

Pisacane failed tragically. It was the old story. In the Bay of Policastro he landed at the village of Sapri, and waited for the promised reinforcements to arrive. Instead of them Bourbon troops appeared, carnage followed, Pisacane fell with a hundred and ten companions, and the colonel of the Neapolitan Cacciatori had all the prisoners shot.

Jessie White was arrested by the Piedmontese in Genoa, Mazzini, who had been there in secret, made good his escape, though both Cavour's and the French Emperor's police searched for him. The British consul in Genoa and then Sir James Hudson in Turin washed their hands of poor Jessie. Cavour told Sir James that he had enough evidence in his possession to condemn her to death or to the galleys. Because of the disturbances Mazzini had started in Genoa when Pisacane sailed, Cavour hoped to catch him and by hanging him get rid of the revolution and its blunders for once and for all. The plots and disturbances would only alienate Napoleon III and the English. Jessie was eventually released, and Mazzini, after being several times on the verge of being caught, got out of Italy, and on arrival in England went to spend a few days in Hastings with the Stansfields. Mr Stansfield reported to Jessie that Pippo (Mazzini) had terribly aged, and was ill and inconsolable on account of Pisacane's death.

VI

While all that took place goody-goody Garibaldi was quietly tilling the soil in Caprera.

Emma Roberts or no Emma Roberts, Garibaldi took with him to Caprera a wench from Nice called Battistina Ravello, the daughter of a seaman, a vulgar creature, yet he seriously considered marrying her. Anyway, she soon produced him a daughter, whom with true delicacy they named Anita. The girl became in time as obstreperous and stubborn as her famous namesake had been.

He had bought one-half of the island for about four hundred pounds. The other half belonged to an English family. Garibaldi and Mr Collins, the Englishman, did not hit it off as neighbours. They had plenty of rows owing to straying pigs and cows, and relations were not improved by young Menotti, who would pelt Mr Collins's cattle with stones. When Mr Collins died in 1864 his widow declared her willingness to sell her half of the island to her unruly neighbours. Garibaldi's English friends, after a good deal of squabbling among themselves, raised the money, and Mrs Collins departed, leaving the Garibaldi household undisputed masters of the rock.

The house Garibaldi built was of one story, whitewashed and flat-roofed, and he built on to it all the time. He worked hard in his garden, which was on the granite rock with only a thin covering of soil over it, held together by brambles and aromatic plants. He built a stone wall round it. In one corner of the garden was a nursery of cypresses, chestnuts, in another vines, and in the middle vegetables. In his bedroom a cord was hung across the room. On the cord were hung his red shirts, drawers and trousers. The bed was hard and narrow; above it in an ebony frame hung a lock of the first Anita's hair. His daughter Teresa had her own room, his friends the Deideris another room, and they all took their meals in the kitchen.

On the shelves of his library stood books on the art of war and navigation, Shakespeare, Byron, works by German freethinkers, the Ethics of Plutarch, Discourses of Bossuet, and the Fables of La Fontaine; and one need not wonder how the works of the Germans reached Caprera; for they were given to him by Mme Schwartz, who now enters his life.

Marie Esperance, the daughter of a Hamburg banker called Brandt, was born in London in 1821, and though very Germanic in the pre-Bismarck sense, she never in the course of her varied existence failed to make use of her British passport. She was brave, a bluestocking, again in the Germanic sense, a vivid writer, but above all very much a woman, which makes her life and work often irritating. She wrote under the name of Elpis Melena (*elpis* in Greek means hope, and *melena* black), and wrote her books in German. She married at the age of sixteen, but her husband soon committed suicide. Then she married Schwartz, a banker like her father, whom she soon divorced. Garibaldi she considered the perfect subject for her pen, consequently she and Dumas did not care for each other, though they both got books out of him. She was after the man Garibaldi too, that is to say, while the writer wanted to write of him the woman wanted to marry him. In her *Recollections and Letters* she does her best to impress on the reader that it was Garibaldi who was keener on marriage than she. That pretension belongs to her afore-mentioned irritating side. Here is a good example of it:

"Only think how you might save the whole family from misfortune," said Signora Deideri to her.

"But what do you mean?" asked Mme Schwartz, somewhat surprised—so she says.

"Surely," said Signora Deideri, "you know that Battistina had a child by the General only five months ago—a child christened Anita Garibaldi after his late wife; that he has promised Battistina to marry her as soon as possible [he was still engaged to Mrs Roberts, which, apparently, was unknown to Mme Schwartz too], that is when he has obtained the certificate of his first wife's death; and, lastly, that he received this very document enabling him to marry again, just before the requiem service in the Piena yesterday?"

"And knowing all these circumstances you can yet think me capable of marrying Garibaldi!" indignantly exclaimed Mme Schwartz, who, one fears, wanted nothing better. "Do you think I would accept happiness and historical renown at the price of perfidy towards a poor woman?" Nevertheless she could not resist remarking in a footnote that the betrothed of others seemed to have had peculiar attractions in the eyes of the great Italian patriot;

for he took Battistina from another man in the manner he abducted Anita.

Signora Deideri pointed out to Mme Schwartz—as if Mme Schwartz could not see it for herself—that Battistina was a low-minded person, and the best thing for the General would be to get rid of her at some small pecuniary expense. "It is too late to discuss Battistina's character," said Mme Schwartz nobly. "She's the mother of a child by Garibaldi, christened after him. Moreover, he has given her a sacred promise of marriage, and this poor woman shall never be plunged into misery through my agency."

Fine words, admirable sentiments, and Mme Schwartz tells the reader in a loud aside: "I will say nothing about the feelings which stirred in me while I uttered these words. I will only add that they were to me as a vow, made solemnly before God and my conscience, to persist in my resolution." Garibaldi married neither of them. On the other hand, Mme Schwartz years later adopted Anita for a pecuniary consideration. This, Battistina accepted because Garibaldi wanted it so. Mme Schwartz sent the girl to be educated in Switzerland. The girl loathed her guts and Mme Schwartz treated her as though she had insisted on taking the horrible girl from her mother out of a lofty sense of duty. In the end the girl returned to her father and died young in Caprera. Generally Mme Schwartz poked her nose into all Garibaldi's affairs, even finding a prospective wife for Menotti, who, however, turned his back on her choice.

Mme Schwartz was an infuriatingly superior person. Describing, for instance, a sea voyage with the Deideris and Garibaldi's legitimate daughter Teresa, who was in the Deideris' care, she wrote: "It would delay me long were I to recount the droll incidents that ensued from the inexperience and impracticality of these worthy natives of Nice. The deathly pallor and pitiable appearance of my three fellow travellers when they left their cabins the following morning, after a rough night, attested only too plainly that they had not been preserved from seasickness by their wise precaution of fastening a large looking-glass upon their naked stomachs."

Of Garibaldi she said, and was not far wrong, that being wholly a man of action and obedient in supreme emergencies to the inspiration of his own genius, he yet was very susceptible to outside influences. She found him by nature inoffensive and credulous, but wanting in that refined tact which "knows how to keep resolutely at a distance all that savours of baseness". That is pretty true if one thinks of the murderer Zambianchi or the poisonous Dr Bertani. She found too that with flattery you could get into his graces because he had a remarkably scant knowledge of mankind. That may be so, but one need not be Garibaldi to be susceptible to flattery. It is a failing shared by great and small. In Garibaldi's case flattery always brought about the same result, namely, his speaking and acting foolhardily against his own better counsel. In him there lived two men: the first the soldier of genius, who knew his strength, could appreciate situations and whose temerity was tempered with admirable level-headedness; the second man was a rumbustious anarchist, an enemy of law and order, a rabble-rouser who would overestimate his strength and turn a blind eye on the situation. Flattery invariably appealed to the second man. The more famous he became, the more he was flattered: the more he was flattered, the sillier the things he did.

Mme Schwartz deplored that her hero should have ended by wrapping himself in a cloak of infallibility, and of his becoming the plaything of partisans. "And surely it is deplorable," she said, thinking of herself, "that

honourable men and ladies of rank, after enduring un-
speakable hardships and dangers, after sacrifices of every
kind, should silently, one by one, have forsaken the hero,
because he could not refuse to listen to the calumnies and
insinuations of these parasites." So she spoke in 1885 when
Garibaldi had been dead for three years.

Her thoughts were different at the time their friendship
began. She gives the date as the autumn of 1853, which, of
course, is a mistake since Garibaldi had not yet returned
from his second exile. 1855 would be more probable. She
sailed in the paddle-steamer *Virgilio* to the island of La
Maddalena. Congratulating herself as usual on being an
excellent sailor, she stood at the stern of the vessel, enjoying
the view of the little port and the fishing smacks at anchor.
Suddenly the captain came up to her and said: "Look!
Garibaldi is coming, and will be on board directly. How
glad I shall be to shake hands with the brave fellow!"

Garibaldi's boat approached with Garibaldi standing
with his right hand on the rigging of the light skiff. His
crew was a sailor and a youth she thought handsome. She
assures us that she looked at Garibaldi not with that fanatical
enthusiasm which idealizes everything, but as one conscious
of his merit, which was the reason that brought her to the
island next to Caprera. And she became quite coy when the
skiff came alongside. She begged the captain not to mention
her to the General. The captain, who must have been a
hard-hearted fellow, did not listen to her entreaties, and
poor Mme Schwartz soon found herself in the ladies'
saloon with the object of her voyage. Coyness left her and
she asked him point blank for certain documents she
needed in order to write a book on him. (She did eventually
write two books: *Denkwürdigkeiten*, 2 volumes, Hamburg,
1860–61, and *Ein Ausflug nach der Insel Maddalena*, so as a
writer she did not waste her time.) She was discouraged

to hear that the documents were no longer with him, but encouraged when Garibaldi, after having spoken of the state of Italy and the Indian Mutiny, asked her to stay with him on his rock. She demurred, and while she demurred she noticed that his was a luminant soul, which is the mark of the chosen of God. She said she would stay at the local inn of La Maddalena.

"But, madam," said Garibaldi, "you cannot possibly stay at that wretched place. You had better come to my house. I am sorry I cannot offer you hospitality worthy of you, but use without reserve whatever belongs to me. I offer it you with all my heart. And now if you will step into my canoe we may be at Caprera before sundown."

She wanted to see La Maddalena first, the globe-trotter that she was, so she went to Caprera only on the following day. Garibaldi came to meet her half way in an elegant canoe. The handsome youth turned out to be Menotti, and when she thanked the General, expressing her regret that she had made him lose so much valuable time, he said: "I have plenty of leisure, for just now I am at war with nothing but stones."

She thought his house looked agreeable because there was simplicity, space and airiness. She noticed a collection of banners, standards and weapons of different countries. She asked Garibaldi to tell her about them, but he changed the subject; for he was not the man to enlarge on his success. Teresa was introduced to her; she took refreshment in the General's room beside a bright fire, and examined his books. Garibaldi himself steered the boat that took her back to La Maddalena, and because she got, as we know, rather mixed up with her dates, she dates his first letter to her 28th November 1857. He calls her Speranza Mia, tells her it was natural for him to love her as she was interested in him. A sweet vision of her used to hover in his imagination, but the reality had enchanted him.

Their friendship flourished, though she spent much time in Rome, she showered presents on him, which included a splendid watch engraved with his initials, she asked him to send Teresa to her, in short she dumped herself into Garibaldi's life. As Garibaldi was quite penniless, there was talk of his taking the command of a merchantman which was to leave for South America. Mme Schwartz promptly suggested accompanying him to look after Teresa during the voyage. Garibaldi decided that going to South America was impracticable for him, and explained to her that in any case his plan had been to leave Teresa behind and in Mme Schwartz's company. Mme Schwartz went to Caprera again. She did not care for it as much as at her first visit. Perhaps she was expecting too much.

Garibaldi's bed, she observed in passing, was so hard that it reminded her of the beds of the orthopaedic institutes. It did not amuse her to have to go to bed at sunset, and before she hardly managed to close her eyes she already heard footsteps, which warned her that it was time to get up. She was not a person to be ordered about; she remained in bed till broad daylight. The windows were curtainless, so while she dressed she was, poor thing, exposed to the gaze of passers-by. She tried to cover the window, but a cow rushed by impetuously, with her head down and her naughty tail in the air, and Mme Schwartz jumped back. It was lucky for her that she stepped back, for Garibaldi and Teresa appeared, one carrying a milk-pail, the other a milking-stool. They would have seen her if she had stayed at the window.

At breakfast Garibaldi apologized for there being so little milk. The reason was that Teresa had thoughtlessly hit the cow in the cowshed, which made the cow unmanageable, and hardly had he begun to milk her than the cow, Zoni by name, upset him, stool and all, and took to her heels. Mme Schwartz related the incident afterwards to Louise Colet, who came to Rome to write her book *L'Italie des Italiens*. In her words: "I related to her this story about his unavailing endeavour to milk his cow for me."

They went for a walk, and under the shade of a luxuriant fig-tree Garibaldi proposed to her. She says a thunderbolt could not have startled her more, nevertheless she gave him an assurance that she would give the matter serious thought. When they continued on their walk Garibaldi suddenly withdrew his arm from hers and said: "The women of the house are very fond of observing everything through a telescope." The only two females on the island were Teresa and the maidservant Battistina, whose relations with Garibaldi she had thought not altogether straightforward already on her first visit. Mme Schwartz describes her as without personal charms, small and ugly. She took her meals with them, and whenever the General showed Mme Schwartz any particular attention, she became passionately jealous. They could not have been congenial meals in spite of Mme Schwartz giving Battistina small presents. Garibaldi's fear lest they should be seen arm in arm convinced her that their relations were far from straightforward, and quoting to herself Terence's "*Homo sum, humanum nil a me alienum puto*", she brought her second visit to an end.

At another visit to Caprera she noticed on board the *Orontes* a woman who was on her way to Garibaldi too. She was an emissary of Mazzini, and the aim of her voyage was to seek Garibaldi's co-operation in an attempt on the life of Napoleon III. That was told to her by Garibaldi himself on her arrival on the island. Garibaldi's

anger at "Mazzini's Jesuitical principles and supposition that
he would advance the federation of Italy by criminal
means was unbounded". Mme Schwartz was deeply
impressed by his noble rage. His face was as red as his shirt,
and when he looked up he said in a voice of thunder:
"Italy shall be united . . . but not by the dagger of an
assassin!"

Their first meeting on the mainland was already in the
great year 1859. Mme Schwartz left Rome, which was
practically her home, with her British passport, which she
says was exceptionally useful for a traveller then, took ship
to Leghorn, had to resign herself to a fourteen hours' stay
in Leghorn, then another steamer took her to Genoa, and
from Genoa it took her four long hours to reach Turin by
train. Garibaldi had arrived there before her.

It was 22nd April and Garibaldi was staying at 31 Via
Lazzaro. When her carriage stopped outside the building
several of the General's followers rushed out, not, however,
to open the door for her, but to hinder her from alighting.
Wherever Garibaldi stayed in Italy his private army
appeared on the spot, turning even his bedroom, if no other
place was available, into its headquarters. The leader and
his bodyguard: how familiar that has become since.

They told Mme Schwartz it was out of the question
for her to see the General, who was overwhelmed with
business, and engaged either with the king or the minister
of war. They turned her away, nevertheless she was back a
few hours later; they were just as adamant in refusing her
entry, but luckily for her one Fruscianti, a faithful Garibaldian, whom she had met in Caprera, ran out on recog-
nizing her voice and took her card, promising it would be
handed to Garibaldi on his return. One need not wonder
what Cavour felt and thought when immediately on his
arrival in Turin Garibaldi surrounded himself with his

private army. It was his private army which made him
generally unpopular in Turin. A number of the adherents
of April 1859 were ex-legionaries of Roman Republican
days.

Mme Schwartz went to her hotel, and sat down to make
bandages for hospital use. Garibaldi came in.

"I confess to you candidly," he said, "that the king has
most favourably impressed me. I have not yet given him
my oath. He has welcomed me with the heartiness of an
old comrade-in-arms. If Italy does not this time shake off
the foreign yoke, she deserves to become the Austrian's
slave."

She asked him whether he had sent for her to entrust
Teresa to her care in case war started with Austria. He said
he had asked her to come simply because he wanted to see
her. Signora Deideri would look after Teresa. In vain one
hopes for some details on his meeting Victor Emmanuel
for the first time. Schwartz the woman records instead that
Garibaldi tried to persuade her to grant his petition, that is
to marry him. She turned the conversation on Battistina.
Garibaldi assured her that Battistina was provided for. He
left five hundred francs with her, which was all the money
he had. Then he took his leave from Mme Schwartz, but
promised to dine with her on the following day.

While history was being made all round her she only
sensed bitter disappointment when Garibaldi sent her a
note saying his rheumatic knee made it impossible for him
to go down the stairs, therefore he was unable to come to
her. "The recollection," she wrote, "of this dolorous and
wintry Sunday would never leave me." Some English
ladies called on her. They were delayed in Turin out of
respect for the Sunday. They asked her to obtain for them
an autograph of Garibaldi. On Monday she remained
indoors, and admits she did not regret it, for Garibaldi

looked in on her for a few minutes. He said he would be back in the evening.

At half past nine she heard a light knock on her door. Twice she said "Come in", but to no purpose. She opened the door and there stood Garibaldi, who had not dared to enter because it was not allowable to visit a lady at such a late hour. She begged the General to go into the adjoining lavatory to freshen himself. On his return she moistened his bronzed hands with Blütthenthau. "Ought I not to be happy," he said, "in thus having my hands perfumed by a lady like you?" She asked him whether he had dined. He took her teacup, and though she wanted to ring for a fresh supply of tea he insisted on drinking tea out of it. Next she gave him a gold chain, which in spite of his opposition she succeeded in fastening to his watch, but he would not allow any part of the chain to show outside his tunic. During the little struggle his wallet fell from his pocket, and picking it up she felt it was too light. So she wanted to give him money.

"You mentioned that you had given Battistina all your money," she said, "and I wager now that you have not a single copper left."

"Wrong," he cried, seizing his pocket book. "It is many a day since I was so rich. For I have but just received a clear thousand francs from the Paymaster of the Forces." He showed her a few bank-notes. After a moment's reflection he exclaimed, "Oh, of course—on my way here I met the Marquis Pallavicini and several comrades-in-arms. These latter were in distress about their families they had left behind them, and so I gave them and certain others the rest."

He asked her to write something at his dictation. He took the paper with him when he left. Only the opening words remained in her memory: "Give a republican a million francs today, and assure yourself that tomorrow he will be a republican no longer."

He promised to dine with her next day, but sent a brief letter instead. "Speranza Mia,—At one o'clock p.m. I set out for Brusasco. I am very sorry not to see you. Write to me there. Heartily yours, G. Garibaldi."

The hour had struck. On the day Mme Schwartz arrived in Turin, that is on 23rd April, Austria sent an ultimatum demanding the disarmament of Piedmont. On leaving the Chamber on that day Cavour, who had regulated the clock that struck, declared: "I am leaving the last sitting of the last Piedmontese parliament—the next will represent united Italy."

VII

Cavour had decided that the war against Austria should take place in 1859, though, naturally, not without some powerful ally. On England's benevolent neutrality he knew he could count, but that would not be enough to oust the Austrians. He had courted France, that is Napoleon III, for several years. The king helped his minister in every possible manner, which included the marriage of his daughter Clotilde to the Emperor's cousin, the un-attractive Prince Napoleon. The shining hour came when Cavour went to Plombières in July 1858 to make a package deal with the Emperor; and it certainly was a package deal. Napoleon promised to liberate Italy from the Alps to the Adriatic, on condition that France would receive Nice and Savoy in compensation for her help. Cavour needed the help, and Napoleon III needed territorial aggrandizement in order to acquire Napoleonic stature before his subjects. So they came to terms.

There were three more matters to be settled. The first was to find a *casus belli*. The Emperor and Cavour put their heads together, reported Cavour to the king, "to run through all the states of Italy to find there that cause for war which was so difficult to discover". They hit on Massa and Carrara, whose inhabitants should be provoked to ask the king for protection and even for annexation of those duchies by Sardinia. Confident of the support of Austria the Duke of Modena would, they hoped, after receiving a haughty and threatening note from Victor Emmanuel, reply to it in impertinent fashion. The king then would occupy Massa and the war could begin.

The next item was the Pope and the King of Naples. Cavour assured the Emperor that it would be easy for the Emperor to safeguard the Pope in quiet possession of Rome while letting the Romagnuols rebel; and as for the King of Naples, there was no need to bother about him unless he chose to come to the assistance of Austria. Cavour took his obstacles one by one. The Emperor was satisfied with his answers.

The third item to be disposed of was the great question: what should be the end of the war? Napoleon's plan at the time was to chase the Austrians to the Isonzo, leave Rome to the Pope together with the surrounding territory, the rest of the States of the Pope would form with Tuscany the Kingdom of Central Italy ruled by the House of Savoy, but there should be no interference with the boundaries of the Kingdom of Naples. The four Italian states would form a confederation, the presidency of which would be given to the Pope. "This arrangement," wrote Cavour to his master the king, "seemed to me entirely acceptable, since Your Majesty, being sovereign by right of the richest and strongest half of Italy, would in fact be sovereign of the whole Peninsula."

Satisfied, Cavour returned to Turin. He had pulled it off, and now all there was left to do was to provoke

8

Austria to war. In December 1858 he assured Odo Russell, who was passing through Turin, that he would force Austria to declare war about the first week in May. As a matter of fact he was about a week out. His accomplice Napoleon III curtly told the Austrian ambassador on 1st January when he received the diplomatic corps that he regretted to find his relations with the Austrian Emperor not as good as he could wish. The Conservative government in England, however, wanted no war against their ally Austria, French public opinion was against it too, and when Napoleon became frightened and joined England in recommending to Piedmont that she should reduce her armies to a peace footing, it seemed to Cavour that he had thoroughly miscalculated; he even thought of committing suicide.

He had one last hope left. France had offered to disarm if Austria did likewise. Perhaps Austria would refuse. So he provoked Austria with every means at his disposal. Austria reacted by refusing to disarm and by sending the ultimatum to Piedmont, for which Cavour longed. Cavour was happy: he had won; England was angry now with Austria: she was not to be feared; the Emperor was well-nigh forced to move now that Austria was the attacker. It was Cavour's masterpiece, the first; the second would be in the following year.

The war did not go precisely as it had been planned at Plombières. The dates speak for themselves:

20th May:	victory of Montebello
30th May:	victory of Palestro
1st June:	crossing of the Tessino
3rd June:	victory of Turbigo
4th June:	victory of Magenta
6th June:	Napoleon enters Milan
8th June:	victory of Marignan

18th June: Napoleon enters Brescia
24th June: victory of Solferino
26th June: crossing of the Mincio
8th July: armistice of Valeggio
12th July: peace of Villafranca.

The Emperor did not liberate Italy from the Alps to the
Adriatic. Many reasons are given why Napoleon III stopped short. The most likely is that he feared Prussia, which
is understandable since his army was deeply involved in
Italy, thus dangerously far from the Franco-Prussian
frontier. Another reason one could accept is that he did not
want the House of Savoy to become too powerful: Italy
had, after all, a common frontier with France. The third
reason one should not dismiss was that he was in a hurry
and aching for a triumphal entry into Paris in the grand
Napoleonic manner. In any case peace was made between
the two emperors in Villafranca; Kossuth cried; Mazzini
was furious for two reasons. The French usurper, monster
and tyrant had liberated Northern Italy from the Austrians
instead of liberation having been left to the idea of *Italia
farà da se*, which for him, of course, meant the revolution,
and Cavour, by bringing in the French usurper with his
bayonets and *chassepots*, had outwitted and outdistanced
the revolution. Cavour resigned when he heard that his
king agreed to the armistice and to the peace treaty. Cavour
almost shouted at him, begging him to continue the
campaign. Victor Emmanuel was more clearsighted that
summer than his great minister. He accepted Villafranca
and Cavour temporarily left office.

Victor Emmanuel did not do badly out of the short
campaign. He received Lombardy, and, after the Zurich
Conference, the duchies of Tuscany, Parma, and Modena,
and the Romagnuols also voted for annexation by Piedmont; and Cavour's prophecy was fulfilled inasmuch

as the king became the most powerful person on the Peninsula.

Garibaldi had come into the picture already in December 1858 when Cavour sent for him. On 20th December he was taken to Cavour secretly by La Farina. It did not transpire what took place at that meeting, though it seems pretty certain that Cavour wanted to make Garibaldi, firstly, harmless by bringing him in on the king's side, and secondly giving him the sort of command in the coming war that would not give Garibaldi a chance to become a nuisance. Cavour was, taking it all in all, dealing with a professed republican and revolutionary, a man who had been sentenced to death by the then king of his country, so he had to take his precautions. At the same time he had a high opinion of Garibaldi the warrior, whose energy he wanted to canalize into a channel in which instead of doing harm he could render the king and Royal Italy signal service.

After his interview with Cavour Garibaldi went to Genoa, where he instructed his old comrade Nino Bixio to start enrolling volunteers among their friends, then returned to Caprera. He came to Turin, saw Cavour again, and Cavour took him to see the king. Garibaldi and Victor Emmanuel got on well immediately, and it could be said that perhaps the king was the only person who ever had power over Garibaldi, and whom Garibaldi truly respected. In the Latin-American sense the king was as much an *hombre* as he; a soldier too, and his personal dignity commanded respect. He did not flatter Garibaldi, remained in his own eyes in all circumstances Garibaldi's king. For him Garibaldi was neither a superman nor a charlatan: he was his conspicuously brave though often recalcitrant subject, whose daredevil exploits nobody admired more than the king. He never used subterfuge with Garibaldi: he struck no attitudes with him, and perhaps those were the reasons why Garibaldi respected him till the end.

Garibaldi was given the command of the Cacciatori delle Alpi. The corps was brought about by enrolling volunteers from all states of the Peninsula, and Italian subjects of Austria were especially welcomed. (To enrol Austrian subjects was part and parcel of Cavour's acts of provocation.) The recruiting office was in Turin, and the Marchese Giorgio Pallavicini was at the head of it. Clandestine agents were sent to the different states to rouse the youth for the patriotic crusade, young men flocked to Turin, and with the town filling up with those patriots one can well understand what Cavour felt like while hoping and praying for Austria to come to his recue by declaring war. There would have been a messy revolution if Austria had failed him.

By the time the Austrian ultimatum came Garibaldi found himself in command of three regiments of infantry beside guides and Genoese sharpshooters. The number of the volunteers increased when he entered Lombardy. For the second time, Lombardy became his battleground; there would be a third time too in 1866. Garibaldi and his staff reached Biella, a mountain town on the Cerra. On 6th May he moved from Biella to Casale, and two days later the first skirmishes with the Austrians took place. The generals of the king's army, like La Marmora and Cialdini, did not think highly of the guerrillero and his Cacciatori. Professional jealousy; but in the king Garibaldi found a staunch ally. The king gave him permission to act independently of the regular army and to make war with his Cacciatori wherever he wanted to, adding: "Go where you like, do what you like. I feel only one regret, that I am not able to follow you." The king's permission suited Garibaldi perfectly: on the other hand neither he nor his

Cacciatori took part in any of the decisive battles of the campaign.

Garibaldi was in his element. He issued a proclamation to the Lombards calling them to arms. "Bondage must cease! He who can seize a rifle and does not is a traitor!" On 23rd May he entered Varese and on the 25th General Urban appeared with an Austrian corps five thousand strong and started shelling the town. Garibaldi counter-attacked. After some hard fighting the Austrians withdrew. That was known as Garibaldi's victory of Malnate, called after the place where the Austrian camp was pitched. Garibaldi moved on towards Como, and stopped at Cavallesca. The ridge of hills between Cavallesca and Como gave him a strategical advantage, not to mention another, also strategical, advantage, namely, that Switzerland was nearby.

General Urban was in San Fermo near Como, showing no desire to attack the Cacciatori. That rather worried Garibaldi. The daughter of the Marchese Raimondi arrived in his camp with letters from the Austrians she had intercepted. Garibaldi gathered that Urban's plan was to cut off his approach to Como, so he decided to attack at once. Though the Austrians outnumbered him by three to one, he threw himself at them with great vigour, and after some hard fighting at bayonet-point the Austrians were driven back. Giving them no respite he pursued them to Como, chased them through the town, and the Austrians left behind ammunition and commissariat carriages, which came in very handy since the regular army had not been overgenerous with supplies.

Como received the liberators with open arms, cheers and flowers. Garibaldi now wanted to know what was happening in the main theatre of war. He sent a telegram to Austrian headquarters in Milan in the name of

General Urban. (It had all been so quick that they could not know yet in Milan that Como was in Garibaldi's hands.) The reply stated that the Franco-Piedmontese had not attacked yet. He dispatched a strong company under Captain Ferrari to Lecco; he himself went back to Varese; for he had heard that General Urban was on his way to attack the town. He arrived at dawn on Monte Sacro near the shrine of the Blessed Virgin. The Austrian lines were below the hills, he sent Giacomo Medici with the advance guard to occupy the Villa Medici, then Garibaldi became aware that he had, with his swift advance, put himself in a precarious position: in fact he was inside a trap. Eventually he wriggled out of it, but that he achieved because luck was with him. It need hardly be mentioned that foolhardy temerity was with him too because with Garibaldi that goes without saying.

General Urban was so pleased and so sure of having Garibaldi where he wanted him that on 4th July he telegraphed Milan assuring headquarters that he would have Garibaldi dead or alive before night fell. Garibaldi first tried a sortie from the Villa Medici, but was repulsed. Then barricades were quickly erected. The Austrians did not interfere: let them do whatever they wanted since they were in the trap. Garibaldi succeeded in having a telegram sent to allied headquarters explaining that he was obliged to fall back and asking for cavalry to support his backward movements. That was a cunning telegram. He knew there was no allied cavalry anywhere for miles around, but as he felt certain that the telegram would fall into Urban's hands, he hoped that Urban would make his dispositions in the belief that he meant to hold his ground. When darkness came Garibaldi made a fine display of bivouac fires, and his men marched up and down before them. His luck appeared in the shape of a noisy thunderstorm and torrents of rain. In the din the guerrillero quietly vanished with all his troops, passing unnoticed near the Austrians, and reached Como just as Urban was getting ready to attack and take the Villa Medici.

Garibaldi was back in Como after what had been described as a "grievous strategical error". A Frenchman, M. Leonce Dupont, who travelled to Como to have an interview with him, left us this picture of him:

> I was introduced in my turn. I experienced some emotion in passing the threshold of a room in which was a man whose adventurous intrepidity had gained such a brilliant renown. At Paris he is endowed with legendary proportions. . . . Everyone dresses him after his own fashion; and of all the costumes I have seen there are few which have not a relationship to a Calabrian brigand. A felt hat and ferocious countenance imbedded in a mass of dishevelled hair, a blouse, and large waistbelt adorned with a dozen cavalry pistols, a naked sabre in his hand; such is the personage of the legend. He may have appeared in this condition ten years ago, under the walls of Rome, but times have changed and Garibaldi with them. The man is small, delicate and nervous, but his small grey eyes flash like polished steel. His hair is cut quite short, and though he wears his beard, it is exactly like hundreds we may see every day in Paris, were it not that it is beginning to turn slightly grey.
>
> I know not if he is cruel, but he has a very kind voice. He is so far civilized that he wears eye-glasses, owing to his short sight. He appears to be about forty, but in reality is fifty-three. He is dressed like all the Sardinian generals in a blue tunic, with silver lace on the collar and cuffs. When I entered he made me sit down by his side, and began by offering me his hand. Then he addressed some very polite remarks to me in the best French I have heard since crossing the Alps. I thanked him for granting me an interview, when he had so many more important matters to attend to, and also told him of the idea

people who had not seen him formed of him. He gave the ghost of a smile, and seemed to care very little what was thought about him.

Another writer, himself a soldier, gives a similar description of Garibaldi in 1859. He had seen him previously in Rome wearing his red shirt, but now found him in a tight general's uniform. The answer of course is that if the Austrians had captured him in a Sardinian general's uniform they would have been compelled to treat him as such. In a red shirt they would have made short shrift with him.

During that campaign some curious tourists took in the war while sightseeing. An Australian gentleman with a fellow colonist and "pastoral squatter" decided on a tour. They took their wives and a young lady friend along, ascended Mont St Gothard with the intention of crossing by the Furka Pass to Interlachen. They found it impracticable, so determined to go to Como to look at the war. Their Swiss guide, on making inquiries among the Swiss soldiery, received the information that it would be highly dangerous to go near such a set of brigands as the Cacciatori. That did not deter the sightseeing party, and an elderly Frenchman whom they met observed that the English might go anywhere, but then so might madmen.

When they reached Como, it was just after lunch; they sent in their cards, and received a message from the aide-de-camp saying that the General was asleep, but that as soon as he woke the cards would be shown to him, and no doubt he would receive the British party. The party pictured Garibaldi tall and large, with sallow complexion and a flowing black beard and the romantic air of those Spanish guerrilla chiefs who sang their own songs to the guitar, or killed people. They were enchanted when they met Garibaldi, who was not like a Spanish guerrilla chief at all—not by a long chalk. He was in fact a quiet un-affected gentlemanly man and he sat down with them. He was deep-chested, powerful without being heavy, and, luckily for him, had a healthy English complexion. His head showed a very fine development, mental as well as moral; his face was good, though not remarkable to a casual observer.

Satisfied, the ladies and gentlemen retraced their steps to Switzerland. When they paid their guide he asked them to recommend him to their friends, and if any of them should want to have a good look at the war he would take them along to the campaign and Garibaldi too. Satisfied with him, they left his name more for future sightseers than posterity. It was Joseph Fettier.

As we are on the anecdotal side, an Englishman should be mentioned, who, according to *The Times* of 29th June 1859, was fifty years old, in Garibaldi's service, carried a Lancaster rifle, and aided by a pair of spectacles of which he stood in need, he brought down every Tyro-lean jaeger he took aim at. Somebody asked him whether he had joined the volunteer corps for the Italian cause or for sport. "I have a great respect for Italian independence," he replied, "but I am also very fond of shooting."

While visitors came and went, the French advanced and the battles of Montebello and Magenta were won. Gari-baldi sent Major Corte to Cavour, who promised ten thousand men well armed and with a battery and a squad-ron of cavalry. He sent only four thousand: they had neither cannon nor horses. Cavour wanted the French and the Sardinians to get all the glory for reasons that are obvious.

Garibaldi, tired of sitting in Como, gathered his volunteers, and by way of Lecco marched on Bergamo. He entered the town four days after the battle of Magenta.

He appeared there with such suddenness that the Austrians, mostly Croats, who had entrained at the station became so frightened that they detrained and took to their heels. On 11th June he moved on against Brescia without any support from the French—another piece of Garibaldian foolhardiness. It came off because the Austrians were retreating along the whole front. He was received enthusiastically in Brescia, issued a proclamation: "Let the glorious Italo-French armies in delivering you from your enemies find you worthy of your liberators", and was loudly cheered.

His next move was to Tre Ponti. Four Sardinian regiments of lancers and two horse batteries under General Sambu were promised him, but did not turn up. Certainly Cavour treated Garibaldi's campaign as of less than secondary importance, which it was; since the war would be won by the French army, and as peace negotiations depended in the end on the two emperors, Garibaldi, victorious or defeated in his small theatre of war, could not have changed anything. On the other hand it was a good thing to keep him on the king's side and occupied.

In spite of the promised reinforcements not turning up Garibaldi attacked at Tre Ponti, and after assaulting them six times he took three positions. It was something of a Pyrrhic victory with the Cacciatori sustaining heavy losses. Garibaldi withdrew, that is fell back on the Franco-Piedmontese main army. The French were not keen on having the Garibaldians with them; Napoleon already had peace in mind; and Garibaldi was sent to the passes of the Stelvio and Tonale, which was conveniently far from the main theatre. On 26th June he sailed up Lake Como after crossing the mountain from Lecco. He took Bormio in a fine attack, and drove the far from numerous Austrians back to the Tyrol. Garibaldi stayed among the mountains indulging in sharp little thrusts till news of the peace of Villafranca reached him. He was furious. He had pictured himself fighting his way into the heart of Austria.

Everybody of the revolution and on the revolutionary fringe loathed the French Emperor, Mazzini first among the haters. Mrs Browning, who had liked Mazzini as much as Mrs Carlyle, now turned against him because of his, for her, unreasonable hatred of the man who had, after all, liberated northern and central Italy; and she expressed the pious hope after the peace of Villafrança that Mazzini might at least be captured and "kept out of mischief".

Garibaldi swallowed, so to speak, his hatred for the moment, though he would spew it up later. At Lovere he issued this Order of the Day, with which he wanted to kill two birds:

> Italians of the Centre: A few months ago we said to the Lombards: "Your brethren of all the provinces have sworn to conquer or to die with you", and the Austrians know whether we have kept our word. Tomorrow we say to you what we then said to the Lombards; and the noble cause of our country will find us serried on the battlefield, willing as we were in the past period, and with the imposing aspect of men who have done and will do their duty.
>
> Returned to your houses, and amid the embraces of your beloved ones, do not forget the gratitude we owe to Napoleon and the heroic French nation, whose valiant sons still lie, for the cause of Italy, wounded and mutilated on the bed of suffering.
>
> Above all do not forget that, whatever may be the intentions of European diplomacy with respect to our destinies, we ought never to detach ourselves from the sacred programme: Italy and Victor Emmanuel!

Garibaldi's last act in the war of 1859 was his resignation as general of the Army of Central Italy, which the king promptly accepted. La Farina, who revived the Societa Nazionale Italiana, he informed that "as long as there remains a foot of our soil to be redeemed we will not lay down our arms". With one foot Garibaldi stepped back into the revolution. The other remained in the king's camp. There would come moments when he would not know exactly where his feet were. Often they were walking on thin ice; at other times on air.

VIII

One of the after-effects of the great summer of 1859 was Garibaldi's marriage to Giuseppina Raimondi, in January 1860. She was eighteen years old, the daughter of the Marchese Raimondi, the same young girl who had come to deliver to him intercepted Austrian letters during the Como campaign. The whole thing was sheer *opera buffa*, and a final lesson for Garibaldi that only simple, preferably fat, daughters of the people were good enough for him.

"In January 1860," says the infuriatingly discreet Jessie White Mario, "Garibaldi married the daughter of the Marquis Raimondi, and, for reasons best left between her and himself, an hour after the ceremony he led her back to her father saying, 'This is your daughter, but not my wife.'"

Biographers of the great man either skimmed over this episode or tried to find some explanation worthy of his greatness. G. E. Curatulo says she never cared for Garibaldi, and was forced into marriage by her father. Garibaldi was madly in love with her, and she was like a vision for him. She, on the other hand, was just as madly in love with Luigi Caroli, who had abandoned her. The wedding was celebrated on 24th January, and in church to boot. As they left the church an anonymous letter was handed to

Garibaldi. There is also a version according to which the anonymous letter was found by Garibaldi in the nuptial bed. Garibaldi asked whether the contents of the letter were true or not. "She confessed but did not vindicate herself." In her memoirs fifty years later Giuseppina declared it was all calumny. (Rumour had it too that she was pregnant by Luigi Caroli.) "I did not love that man," she wrote of Garibaldi, "and on our wedding night that man came precisely to tell me: 'Fear not, I won't take you.' I had to sacrifice myself for the ideal which for every woman is the dearest and most precious. I believed I had to do that in silence, and in silence I did it for fifty years."

In his *Memorie* Garibaldi relates that on 3rd December 1859 he received a letter from that "bella fanciulla", which gave a new meaning to his existence. When he saw her he pointed out to her that he was poor, old, melancholy by nature, and spoke even of the ties that bound him to other women. She replied that she had considered all that.

Naturally, Mme Schwartz gives her version too. The newspaper in which she read of the marriage fell straight from her hands. A year later she talked of it with Garibaldi and Signora Deideri. It appeared that she, Giuseppina Raimondi, had not only deceived Garibaldi criminally by accepting his hand after having given herself to another by whom she was already pregnant, but she went even so far as to make a date with her lover on the very day of the marriage. The lover was an officer of Garibaldi's own troop. When he heard that his adored general was going to marry his mistress he wrote to him exposing his own relationship with the girl. The letter did not reach Garibaldi.

The shameful connection between Giuseppina and her lover was condoned by the Raimondi family (if one believes Mme Schwartz). Giuseppina used to put her letters to her lover into a casket on the chimney-piece, and they were regularly collected and forwarded by a servant. On the eve of her marriage Giuseppina quarrelled with her brother, who, in order to revenge himself, took one of her love-letters from the casket, and gave it to Garibaldi after the wedding. With the paper in his hand Garibaldi went from room to room in the villa looking for his pistols. He did not find them, so he went to his wife's room.

"Have you written this letter?" he asked, putting it before her.

She acknowledged that she had. It is a pity that neither Mme Schwartz nor the Signora Deideri reproduce her answer.

"Then see that you do not bear my name. I leave you for ever," he said.

"Ah!" exclaims Mme Schwartz, "would that the blue waves of the Tyrrhenian Sea, over which the *Sardegna* [Mme Schwartz was passenger on board on her way back from Caprera] glided so smoothly that evening, had been a Lethe in which I could have drowned the remembrance of this tragic episode in the life of the Italian hero!" That pious wish did not stop her, however, from publishing for posterity the tragic episode.

According to her, Giuseppina went to La Maddalena in 1861 to see Garibaldi. He refused to see her. All Curatulo relates is that she asked after Garibaldi's health when he was wounded at Aspromonte. Garibaldi tried hard to get his marriage annulled. It is reported that Victor Emmanuel observed, with one eye, one supposes, on Contèssa Millefiori with whom he led an exemplary extra-conjugal life, that if it were possible he would be the first to avail himself of it. Nevertheless Garibaldi, since the marriage was not consummated, got his annulment on 14th

January 1880, to enable the old man to marry another servant girl, Francesca Armosino, who had already given him three children, one son and two daughters; Clelia, the eldest of them, was born in 1867, Rosita in 1869 (she died in 1871), and Manlio, the son, in 1873.

Francesca is described as sturdy and ugly: so was Battistina. Francesca came to Caprera in 1866 as nursery maid to the children of Garibaldi's daughter Teresa, who was married to the very left-wing Canzio of Genoa. When the Canzios left the island they wanted to take the nursery maid back with them. Garibaldi would not let her go, and Clelia was born in the following year. Mme Schwartz said the child was pale and not at all pretty. When at long last he was able to marry her the ceremony was performed by the mayor of La Maddalena, who came to Caprera for the purpose. The Canzios and Menotti with his wife Italia Bedeschini-Garibaldi were present at the wedding. It is again Mme Schwartz who tells us that the General's face shone with joy, that he sat in his rocking-arm-chair like the patriarch he was by then, was wrapped in a poncho as white as snow, and wore a red handkerchief round his neck. Francesca was dressed in white. Garibaldi gave his occupation as a husbandman, and among the telegrams of congratulation was one from King Umberto I. But all that is still a long way off.

Luigi Caroli went off to fight in Poland after Giuseppina's marriage to Garibaldi, was taken prisoner by the Russians and sentenced to twelve years' hard labour and perpetual exile in Siberia. There he died, and with him dead one could almost say that where Garibaldi was concerned his second marriage never existed. So we can return to Garibaldi of 1859, and Mme Schwartz is once more our guide.

Garibaldi wrote to her after the war from Lovere on

6th August, calling her a refined, affectionate and sympathetic soul. Writing from Modena on the 23rd he said his position was so uncertain that he dared not say she should come. She insisted on seeing him, and he told her in his next letter that he was still in Modena, but if she did not find him there she would be told where he was. Garibaldi was on his triumphal tour. When Mme Schwartz with the Deideris and Garibaldi's daughter Teresa arrived in Modena, they found that he and his retinue had moved on. Signora Deideri always dressed the fifteen-year-old Teresa in black, we gather, whereas she herself dissimulated her twelve lustres with white transparent garments, decked to the waist with little *volants*. "Now it happened," says Mme Schwartz, "that one of these garments and sundry other less ethereal things had been entrusted to the washerwoman," when a telegram arrived from Garibaldi instructing the little party to join him at Ravenna. There was no time to get hold of the washerwoman, so poor Signora Deideri had to abandon the garments and the less ethereal things. She rushed round the place shouting, sobbing and wringing her hands. "*Figie mie, figie mie*," she shrieked in the vulgar dialect of Nice, "*mi veste, le lingé!*" That all goes to show that Mme Schwartz had to put up with a lot for her general's sake.

She had more trouble on the journey with the good people from Nice, but Ravenna was reached and they were received by the General himself, who showed them up to their rooms. At dinner Mme Schwartz met the Marchese Rora, the political delegate from Turin. The populace shouted and cheered outside the palace, and the marquis encountered some difficulty in overcoming Garibaldi's modesty and taking him out on the balcony. Mme Schwartz frequently emphasizes his modesty in the course of his tour. She probably thought that necessary so as

9

to stop simpletons asking themselves why the tour was necessary.

On the next day they went on an excursion with the General. Mme Schwartz was in the first carriage with Garibaldi, Signora Deideri and Teresa. He spoke to her of the late war and his campaign, which he called magnificent. They arrived at the house of the steward of the Marchese Guiccioli, and on being shown into a humble room Mme Schwartz discovered that they were in the identical refuge "where Madame Garibaldi breathed her last sigh on the bosom of her sorrowing husband, a true victim of heroism and conjugal love". Eighteen guests sat down to a table loaded with delicacies in the room where Anita died. Garibaldi made a stirring speech to the assembled company. Italy, he said significantly, must be freed from the Alps to Sicily. Not for a moment, one sees, did Garibaldi consider the peace of Villafranca more than an armistice.

After the repast the party went to a modest chapel and, led to a recess by the altar, Mme Schwartz knew instinctively that Anita's ashes reposed there. The return journey took them through the hamlet of San Antonio. During the retreat from Rome in 1849 a poor cobbler of San Antonio gave Garibaldi refuge. Now the man was too sick to leave his bed: Garibaldi paid him a visit: the cobbler was so strongly affected with joy by the visit that he recovered from his illness. Garibaldi had become a miracle-worker, which is not surprising for a man who took to baptizing babes. He baptized them in the name of God and Jesus the Legislator.

Mme Schwartz mentions in an aside that Jessie White Mario used to be Mrs Roberts's maid, then talks of Battistina, then moves on to Bologna with the General. In the midst of deafening shouts and tumultuous demonstrations they set out in a carriage, Garibaldi silent with displeasure because she sat beside Teresa, that is not beside him. Suddenly Garibaldi jumped over her and Teresa and landed on the coachman's box. The coachman was amazed but the General's temper improved. He tapped Mme Schwartz lightly on the shoulder and asked softly: "You understand Spanish, do you not?" Of course she understood Spanish. "Well, then," he said, "I will sing you a Spanish song, and you must translate it to prove that you understand it."

He sang in a melodious tenor an Andalucian romance; the words Mme Schwartz forgot, though remembered its general tendency. It was about a certain majo who, believing he had offended his morena, craved her pardon. She says she mentions the episode only as a proof of Garibaldi's extraordinary vivacity; but supposing that the morena he had in mind was Giuseppina Raimondi?

They were at the Hotel Brun in Bologna, Garibaldi surrounded by his partisans, old and new, petitioners and military men of all ranks. When political business was not very urgent Mme Schwartz amused the company on a spinet. Medici, Cosenz and Nino Bixio were in the company. The General showed her two splendid banners, which, he was given to understand, the young daughter of the Marchese Raimondi had embroidered for him. "Do you think that such work can come from ladies' hands?" he asked. Mme Schwartz immediately disabused him. No ladies' hands could have done such work: it had surely been manufactured.

During the meal that followed she noticed that Garibaldi used a ragged object with a big hole in it as a handkerchief. "Perhaps one of the gentlemen will be so good as to buy me a pocket-handkerchief," he remarked; and after dinner Mme Schwartz went straight out to buy a stock of handkerchiefs for the General. That handkerchief with the hole in it has been held up down the years as another proof of Garibaldi's disinterestedness and modesty. The answer might be that he cared neither one way nor the other for holes in handkerchiefs. In the following year in Naples he went in state to the Opera in a faded red shirt, yet at the same time he was spending huge sums of public money without thought or care; and plenty of fuss was made of his refusing to incur the expense of a new coat for his own use. This writer at least thinks that refusing a new shirt was not subtle propaganda: it was the way Garibaldi was made. His enemies could not help comparing his behaviour in Naples to Cavour's. When Cavour became finance minister he sold all his stocks and shares without telling anyone.

Still harassed in Bologna by Signora Deideri's disclosures about Battistina, Mme Schwartz decided to return to Rome. By his daughter Teresa Garibaldi had a costly ring delivered to Mme Schwartz; but when she wanted to know why the General did not come to say goodbye to her, Teresa told her, "with the coolness she inherited from her father", that he was well aware that she was going but had gone to bed. However, she did succeed in seeing him, and she discovered that he had only one pair of boots, they pinched, and he was without slippers. She promised to embroider a pair of slippers for him when she reached Florence *en route* for Rome. He thanked her, kissed her hand, but did not press her to postpone her departure. So she went and was treated on her way with the respect due to "the English lady who was with Garibaldi".

In Florence she received a telegram from Garibaldi asking whether she was still there. If so, he had an important communication to make. On 5th October a letter arrived in which he asked his Speranza if she could go to

Messina on a delicate mission. "Yes" was her telegraphed
reply, and she asked whether she should return to Bologna.
"This afternoon at four o'clock a person leaves Bologna to
consult with you in Florence," Garibaldi telegraphed.
Mme Schwartz was in great agitation. What was it all
about? Who was the person charged with the message?
When at last a knock came on her door after a sleepless
night, she expected it to open on someone like Medici,
Cosenz, Bixio or Deideri. To her horror she beheld a
woman entering her bedroom. The woman was pretty,
about thirty-five, and dressed elegantly in black. Mme
Schwartz thought it was some mistake.

It was not. The woman handed her a letter from the
General. "The bearer is a sincere friend of Italy: she is
commissioned by me to impart a scheme to you. You may
thoroughly confide in her." Mme Schwartz asked the lady
for information. She said she knew nothing, and only
after Mme Schwartz threatened to write to Garibaldi
asking for more explicit information did she unpin from
the inner lining of her dress another small paper. "Go to
Messina," Garibaldi commanded, "find the English consul
there, come to an understanding with the committee, put
them in communication with me and with the committee
in Palermo. Be cautious! But proceed boldly towards the
goal, because the matter will have a fortunate issue." The
stranger then produced a third piece of paper in the
General's handwriting. "The mission with which I
charge you is sacred, but very dangerous. . . . Before
undertaking it make a serious estimate of your strength.
. . . If you accept it, remember there is much to be done
not only in Sicily, but also in Naples and Rome. . . ."

After some hesitation, and feeling exceedingly disturbed,
Mme Schwartz accepted the assignment. She was accompanied by the fair stranger whom she could not bring

herself to trust. She told Mme Schwartz that she was a
widow, and entrusted her with one more piece of paper,
which contained an insurrectionary appeal from Garibaldi
to the Sicilians. They took a steamer to Messina, and
Mme Schwartz's beautiful little greyhound sailed with
them. The steamer was the *Vatican*, and the captain was
strikingly handsome. The widow got off with him at once,
one more reason, thought Mme Schwartz, to get rid of
her, which she did in Naples where the *Vatican* called
after Civitavecchia. Mme Schwartz got rid of her by
giving her a letter of introduction to the Prince Colonna.
"The prospect," she explains, "of exchanging a ship's
captain for a prince had its desired effect." The two ladies
never met again, though Mme Schwartz learnt in time
certain facts about her, which were deeply deplorable and
threw into the shade her starlight revels on board the
Vatican.

On arrival in Messina the customs officers were not
friendly; for the Bourbon officials were convinced that
every Englishman was an emissary of the unpleasant,
prying Mr Gladstone. She went first to an hotel, where
they could give her only a large bedroom with partitions
instead of the bedroom and small sitting-room she needed;
then she went to the consulate. The vice-consul, a Mr
Richards, was not in, so she left her card, and he soon came
to see her. She had been expecting an Englishman, but she
was shocked to see that the man was a Levantine. She was
even more shocked when it transpired that Mr Richards
wanted to have nothing to do with her mission. She
pressed him to declare his political opinions. "Madame,"
he said, "if you suppose that Her Majesty Queen Victoria
will favour a revolution in Sicily on behalf of your friend
Garibaldi, you are mightily in error."

In her subtle fashion Mme Schwartz reached the conclusion that Mr Richards had thus expressed himself only to draw her into an avowal, and she looked forward eagerly to the morrow, for he promised to call on her again. She stayed indoors, none the less the Levantine did not keep his word. She wrote to him, asking for an appointment. In his reply he said he would give himself the pleasure of calling on her the next day: and call he did, giving her her passport and telling her not to set foot in the consulate again.

She decided to return home. Garibaldi had evidently been misinformed about Mr Richards's tendencies. But there was no ship before the 17th October. That meant three nights of waiting. She lay down at night in her Tunisian caftan, lapsing into a dozing condition, fancying that she might at any moment hear the cry of "Death to the Bourbons! Long live Victor Emmanuel and Garibaldi!" Instead a peremptory voice ordered her to open the door in the name of authority. She swallowed Garibaldi's proclamation to the Sicilians, it nearly choked her, then three disagreeable fellows broke down the door and arrested her. They told her they knew why she had come and what she was about. In vain she pointed out that she was a British subject. They took her to a terrible prison, and cast her into a foul dungeon, the walls of which were of unhewn stone, streaked with lines of damp; the furniture consisted of a dirty sack of straw, a wooden stool and an earthen water-jug. She found herself buried alive; and the reader of her *Recollections* cannot help asking himself: now, how on earth is she going to get out?

It was simple. The gaoler turned out to be a friendly soul. After she had endured for hours the pangs of one under sentence of immediate death the gaoler aroused her from her delirium and said: "Signora, I may be a stranger to you, but you are not so to me. Some time back you used to spend the summer at Sorrento where I was born. You may perhaps remember—though it must be eight or nine years ago—a certain day when you were walking by yourself from Sorrento to your villa, and you were overtaken by three men running at full speed, and who, thinking only of themselves, called out to you, 'Run! Run!' What was the matter? Why, just this: an ox, half mad with rage, had got loose from the slaughter-house, and was tearing down the road upon you. You were weak and unwell then, and could not possibly make haste . . . you were looking about you in mortal terror, not knowing what to do, when you saw a little old woman running after you, not like those selfish men, to save herself only, but to do her best for you, and help you to a yard close by, where there was a great myrtle tree, often visited by strangers. She had no sooner got you there and closed the door, than the ox rushed furiously by. . . ."

The gaoler was the old woman's son and, to cut a long story short, he extricated her, that is he got her out of dungeon and prison, took her to his little house, and later got her on board the *Quirinal* and she sailed to Naples; and the reader is left wondering whether to believe a word of it. "I shall always be deeply grieved to think," she says, "that my noble deliverer was destined to enjoy the fruits of my lifelong gratitude for so short a time. Some years later when the cholera visited Sicily and ravaged Messina, Peppo, his wife and child all fell victims to the dreadful epidemic." Thus no witness was left alive when she published her *Recollections*. The first half of the story, however, goes to show Garibaldi's irresponsibility where plans and projects were concerned.

She saw Garibaldi in Bologna on her return. She recounted her terrible adventures. "I had thought as much," he said calmly. When she told him of her miraculous escape, he said: "You are well out of it." Then he patted her shoulder, and called her the bravest of the brave, who had the best right to wear the red shirt. Then he changed the conversation.

She was staying in a simple inn, the Pelican. Garibaldi did not propose that she should move to the palace of Prince Albergati where he was staying. She guessed the reason: he did not want even his own entourage to know of her presence in Bologna. But he came to dine with her at the Pelican. The food was good: food, however, was always good if Mme Schwartz was the hostess. He told her he would be leaving Bologna in the evening, though not before saying farewell to her. He did not turn up, she went to bed, there was a knock on her door, she called out, there was no answer, the knocks continued, she called out primly: "I shall open to no one who does not declare himself." Three gentlemen wished to see her. She adjusted her toilette thinking they came from Garibaldi. The three entered. One of them was a Hungarian.

They wanted to see Garibaldi on an important, urgent matter, and wished her to arrange an interview, in fact had thought he might be with her. She said it was impossible since Garibaldi had left at six for Rimini.

"Not so," said the Marquis X—, "for I have just seen him picking his teeth at the table in the Hotel Brun where he was supping."

They insisted that for Italy's sake she should arrange the interview. She promised to stay up till half past ten; the gentlemen decided to wait at a nearby café. Shortly after they had left, a letter was delivered to her from the General, excusing himself for not having come, and asking her to write to him if she had anything to communicate. She let the three gentlemen know that she could not be useful in bringing about a meeting. They still insisted, and eventually Mme Schwartz went to the Palazzo Albergati, which she reached at midnight. She found no sentry, not even a porter. Guided by a feeble moon she mounted the stairs, saw that the second floor was carpeted, so climbed up to it. She found herself in a vast anteroom, through which two wax candles shed a light. She advanced through wide passages lighted by Carcel lamps. In the neighbourhood of statues, clocks, curtains of thickest damask and sofas were troopers' hats, sashes, pistols, red jackets and sabres, all in the most motley confusion. It seemed to her that the princely luxury of the palace protested against the ruthless arms. On a secretaire she saw a mountain of torn letters and telegrams: Garibaldi could not be far. She was challenged at last. The man knew her and called her signora; for, she explains, with the Garibaldians signora was her only designation. He told her to go straight into Garibaldi's room.

She found him on a richly gilded bed in his red shirt and white poncho reading newspapers of different countries. He was angry when she told him what her errand was. Gentlemen should not disturb a lady at night. He took up the illustrated paper he was reading and said: "See now, how these English concern themselves with me! By God! all the history of my life, my fighting adventures, even those of South America, mine and my Anita's difficulties: it is all given on the stage of Astley's theatre, and now depicted in these papers. What people they are!"

When she took leave of him he said: "Write to me; write to me, wherever you are."

"Can a man exalted to the clouds," she thought, "by an entire nation, like this man, cause a single devoted woman such suffering at heart?"

The proposal of the three gentlemen was a *coup d'état* in

Rome and the assassination of Cardinal Antonelli. Garibaldi refused to have anything to do with it.

Soon Garibaldi returned to Caprera.

IX

The cession of Savoy and Nice, but especially Nice his native town, filled Garibaldi's simple heart—simple in matters of politics and statesmanship—with blazing fury. He did not bother even to glance at the advantages that accrued to Italy thanks to the ceding of Nice. It was his cradle, etc. He seemed to have forgotten that Nice was French when he was born. The king lost his cradle too, namely Savoy. His reaction was different. "After giving my daughter to France," he said, "they may as well take the cradle."

Garibaldi became deputy for Nice a week before the annexation was signed. Garibaldi appeared in the Chamber in Turin: Cavour was prime minister again. Garibaldi did not care for parliaments and did not think much of them; but he did care to put a spoke in Cavour's wheel whenever he had a chance. At the moment Cavour entered the Chamber Garibaldi called out loudly: "*Domando la parola!*" Then he asked leave to put a question. Cavour moved the previous question, and said the Chamber was not properly constituted yet; moreover, he would not answer Garibaldi. Two deputies rose to support Garibaldi, pointing out that the Chamber had been sworn in on the previous Monday, besides the king had already addressed the members. What more was necessary? Plenty, with Cavour present. Rattazzi intervened in the debate, Cavour followed with a long argument on parliamentary precedent, and having, so the Garibaldians believed, confused the Chamber, a division was taken and the previous question was adopted by a large majority.

Garibaldi tried again in the Chamber on 12th April. He had been primed, and read out the fifth article of the constitution, according to which no sale or barter of any part of the kingdom could take place without the consent of parliament. His speech had been written for him. In his speech he asked for the plebiscite of Nice to be postponed till the treaty, of which the cession of Nice was a consequence, had been debated in the Chamber. He denounced the treaty of cession of 24th March as an infraction of the old charter of Nice and a violation of the right of nationality.

Now Cavour, who had listened to him and in whose subtle mind his second masterpiece was shaping, and in which masterpiece Garibaldi would have a part assigned, did not care for Garibaldi's speech. Yet he left to Garibaldi the pleasures of losing one's temper, which Garibaldi promptly did when his motion was defeated. "The true ground for it [the treaty] is that the treaty is an integral part of our policy," Cavour said in his speech, "the logical and inevitable consequences of a past policy, and an absolute necessity for the carrying out of this policy in the future." There was practically nothing ambiguous in those words, yet Garibaldi did not twig. In great anger he left the Chamber and was chaired by his supporters.

The man who had prompted his second speech was an English journalist, Laurence Oliphant. Because he was English he was considered by Garibaldi and his followers an expert on constitutional procedure even in a foreign country with its own foreign procedure. Having failed in parliament Garibaldi decided on direct action, which was more to his liking and suited to his temperament. "Always interpellations," he sneered when Oliphant advised him to try in the Chamber again. Garibaldi formed a Nizzard committee, and decided to take ship from Genoa to Nice, and to smash the ballot boxes on arrival.

They entrained in Turin for Genoa, Oliphant travelling with them, and in his special compartment Garibaldi spent his time reading and tearing up letters. On arrival in Genoa Oliphant was sent to hire a diligence for the party. When he left the diligence office he went to report to Garibaldi at his hotel. It was a second-rate place, a number of young men were at the door, and Oliphant was allowed in only after his name was taken. He was shown into a dining-room where more than twenty people were supping, with Garibaldi at the head of the table. Garibaldi made him sit down beside him, then told him he was sorry but he would have to abandon the Nice project (as if Oliphant had urged him to go and smash the ballot boxes). The gentlemen at the table, he explained, were all from Sicily, had come to meet him and had told him that the moment was ripe to invade Sicily. Fond as he, Garibaldi, was of his native city, he could not sacrifice those greater hopes of Italy to it.

Thus the fracas at Nice came to nought, and the first half of Cavour's second masterpiece came into operation.

Cavour wanted Sicily and Naples for his king and Italy. The Kingdom of the Two Sicilies was as Italian a kingdom as Piedmont. The Neapolitan Bourbons might be riddled with faults, but Italians they had been for a long time, and even Cavour could not invent foreign domination since there was none. If His Majesty in the south had some Swiss troops, then His Majesty in the north had Hungarians. It was out of the question to make a headlong attack on Naples. The Papal States, or what was left of them, were between the north and the south. That would not have worried Cavour. Napoleon III would not have stood for an attack on Francis II. That worried Cavour.

Taking almost a leaf out of Mazzini's book he tried to instigate rebellion in Naples, but in spite of the Bourbon king's misrule he got nowhere with it. Sicily was the gateway to Naples, and Sicily was always in ferment. Still, sending the king's troops to take Sicily was out of the question, once more because of Napoleon III. Therefore some other method should be used to invade the territory of a friendly power. Cavour's choice fell logically on Garibaldi, for Garibaldi was the ideal man for a *coup de main*; the people would, contaminated as it were by his intrepidity and enthusiasm, follow him anywhere. Garibaldi's reputation ensured that one could pretend he did it all on his own bat, and if he failed, which was very possible, one could wash one's hands of him. If he succeeded and became too big for his seven-league boots, then the second half of the master plan would be put into operation. From the moment his scheme had matured in his head Cavour threw overboard all ethical considerations, if he ever had any, where unification of Italy under the king his master was concerned. It was fortunate for him and Victor Emmanuel, and very unfortunate for insipid, useless Francis II, that Lord Palmerston, of whom Cobden said he was absolutely impartial, having no bias, not even towards the truth, was at the time prime minister of England, and Lord John Russell his foreign secretary.

On 6th April, in fact shortly before Garibaldi's appearance in the Chamber in Turin, General Fanti of the king's army wrote to General Ribotti, also of the regular army, asking him in Cavour's name whether he would be willing to resign his commission in the army if revolution broke out in Sicily and to go there. Ribotti was keen, and went to Turin, but by then Cavour had Garibaldi already in mind, so nothing came of that. Moreover, Cavour knew that Garibaldi had Sicily in mind, and had not only written to Milan to the Directors of the Million Rifles Fund for arms and money, but was already recruiting companions in Genoa, for a descent on Sicily.

Garibaldi went to see the king, who was still hesitant. The king, some days later, refused his request to take along Sacchi's regiment. The king certainly did not want it to be said abroad that regular troops of his took part in an adventure of which he pretended he had never heard. Garibaldi moved to Genoa, where preparations began on a big scale, and soon all Europe knew about it, including Naples, yet Naples did absolutely nothing to prepare itself for it. Cavour went to Bologna to see the king. Many versions were given later of what took place at their meeting, though one thing is evident: no obstacles were put in Garibaldi's way to attack at his own risk the king's *bon frère* of Naples in Sicily.

There was one man who believed in old-fashioned morals. That was the Marchese Massimo d'Azeglio, the governor of Milan, who forbade any of the twelve thousand firearms to be taken from the armoury for the Million Rifles Fund, that is for Garibaldi's expedition to Sicily. He refused because he believed one should not arm guerrilla bands against a power that continued to have friendly diplomatic relations with the court of Turin.

They were getting worried in Genoa because the arms were not arriving, so Dr Bertani, who was on Garibaldi's committee, sent Francesco Crispi to Milan. When he heard of d'Azeglio's refusal he went to see the minister of the interior, who told Crispi that he would not help. At the same time he advised Garibaldi in a roundabout way that fifteen hundred rifles might be obtained from the National Society. La Farina was its secretary, and Cavour had told him before his departure for Tuscany that those arms could be used for the invasion of Sicily. Garibaldi received his rifles, which were old smooth-bore muskets, converted from flint-locks into percussion, and sold as obsolete by the army, very different from the new Enfield rifles, with which d'Azeglio refused to part. Such trifles could not bother Garibaldi on the eve of the finest adventure of his life.

Victor Emmanuel, with Cavour at his elbow, wrote to Francis II, drawing his attention to the fact that Italy could now be divided into two powerful states of the north and the south, which, if they adopt the same national policy, may uphold the great idea of the times: national independence; but to achieve that it would be necessary for his Sicilian Majesty to abandon the course he had held hitherto. The principle of dualism could still be accepted by Italians. A threat followed: the last thing Victor Emmanuel wanted was that Francis II should experience the bitterness of the terrible words—too late.

That letter was rather sent, as Dr Trevelyan himself puts it, for the satisfaction of the king's and Cavour's consciences, and for the edification of Europe and of posterity, than for the benefit of Francis II.

Garibaldi had dreamed of invading Sicily for a long time; but he dreamed of returning to Rome all the time. With men like Bertani in his entourage it did not appear impossible to Cavour that instead of Sicily Rome might become his destination—or both. Rome was out of the question, not out of respect for the Holy Father, but in fear of the French Emperor, whose troops garrisoned the Holy City. He was on tenterhooks till the expedition was well on its way to Sicily. In fact he had told an emissary of Garibaldi that if there were an expedition to the Marches the government would oppose it by every means in its power.

Things were not going smoothly in Genoa. News had come from Sicily. The insurrection had been suppressed in Palermo. Garibaldi said with tears in his eyes on receiving the news that it would be folly to go. Though Victor Hugo considered Pisacane a greater man than Garibaldi, probably because he had failed, Garibaldi did not want to follow in the wake of his and other tragic failures. He was willing to take any risk, but only if there was a chance, even if it was no more than one in a hundred. Mazzinians in Genoa were saying Garibaldi was afraid. Nino Bixio was ready to start with La Masa without Garibaldi, nevertheless Garibaldi made his decision only after he was assured that the insurrection had been revived in the mountains above Palermo. (After all, it was in Genoa that he had learnt as a youth what it is like when no insurrectionists turn up.)

They sailed from Quarto on 5th May. They sailed in two ships, the *Piedmonte* and the *Lombardo*. Garibaldi was on the *Piedmonte*. The first stop was Talamone. Zambianchi, the murderer of priests in 1849 in Rome, was armed by Garibaldi there, and sent by him to attack the Papal States. Zambianchi started off in the hope, which Garibaldi shared, of raising an insurrection. Garibaldi seriously believed that nothing could be easier, and once the rising took place Bertani and Medici would send reinforcements to Zambianchi from Genoa. It ended in failure. When they recrossed the frontier Zambianchi was arrested, kept in prison till February of the following year, then banished to America. He died on the voyage.

The organization of the Thousand was completed in the bay of Talamone. The exact number was 1089, including four Hungarians. One of them was General Türr. The peacetime occupations of the Thousand were as follows: 150 lawyers, 100 doctors, 50 engineers, 30 sea captains, 20 chemists, the rest were scientists, artists, teachers, merchants, one woman, Rosalia Montmasson, but not a single peasant. Garibaldi formed them into eight companies of infantry, artillery, twenty-three guides but without horses, and Genoese carabineers. They did not treat the population of Talamone too well, and refused to obey their officers. Garibaldi was sent for. He came from the *Piedmonte* and ordered the lot to embark. They obeyed.

Nino Bixio, who was a sort of General Paton of the expedition, was sent to the coal stores. He seized and shook the official till he handed him the keys of the coal-shed. The *Piedmonte* and the *Lombardo* left Talamone on 9th May. Bixio was in charge of the troops on the *Lombardo*. He threw a plate at a corporal whose reply he found insolent, then paraded the troops and told them if they dared to shrug their shoulders or thought of mutiny he would cut them to pieces.

There was no need for such talk in the *Piedmonte*. Garibaldi was in great fettle, and in his deck-cabin he sat and composed verses about tyranny and revolt. Next morning there was no sail in sight. They were well away.

With all the noise, preparations and comings and goings France, naturally, took notice. Besides, there still was the fear of Garibaldi going for Rome instead of Sicily. On 7th May Cavour telegraphed the governor of Cagliari in Sardinia informing him that Garibaldi had sailed with four hundred volunteers for Sicily. If he entered a port in Sardinia he should be arrested with his whole expedition. If necessary he should use the squadron commanded by Admiral Count Persano. Next day Cavour telegraphed again. Garibaldi should not be arrested out at sea, only if he entered a port. On 10th May, having heard that Garibaldi was at Talamone, and now really fearing an attack on the Papal States, he sent a battleship there with the order that the Thousand should be arrested if still there. But the Thousand had sailed on that day.

On 23rd May Cavour told Ricasoli, the Iron Baron of Tuscany, that he agreed with his opinion that it would be wrong as well as dangerous to put obstacles in Garibaldi's way because of the enthusiasm of the country for his patriotic enterprise. France, he added with a sigh of relief, showed less displeasure than he expected.

The rest now depended on Garibaldi.

III

THE THOUSAND

I

THE morning sun warmed the pretty little town of Marsala in Sicily. An English corvette lay at anchor near the entrance to the port, facing the warehouses of the English wine-shippers of Marsala. In the distance one could see a couple of steamers, men-of-war of the Neapolitan Navy. They had been in the port on the previous day. Today was 11th May. A few fishing smacks came into port and discharged their catch. Some hours later two steamers hove into sight. They seemed to be on their way to Malta; but after passing the Neapolitans on the port side they turned straight towards the harbour. When it became evident that the two vessels were coming into port the curious and the loafers went to the end of the pier to have a better look at them.

The two vessels approached. No flags, but apparently large crews, for the decks were crowded with human beings. The English corvette signalled to them, receiving, however, no response. The Neapolitan men-of-war turned towards the harbour too. The two strange vessels were approaching fast. Though they had not replied to the English corvette's signals, the English, so it looked, were well aware of the intentions of the two newcomers, since the officers and crew stood quietly on deck watching with calm curiosity the approaching ships. A launch was got ready to go and meet the incoming strangers. A Neapolitan officer appeared with a few soldiers. The garrison of

Marsala consisted of about a hundred men. A small crowd assembled, windows filled with the curious. When the first of the two vessels passed the light tower, the crowd broke into a panic, and men, women and children de-camped. Somehow they had sensed imminent danger. Soon one could read the name of the first vessel: *Piedmonte*. A launch left her the moment she dropped anchor and came alongside the pier. After a few words were exchanged with the loafing fishermen and sailors, the launch returned to the *Piedmonte*, then fishermen and sailors jumped into their boats and rowed out to the *Piedmonte*. Disembarkation began at once. The *Lombardo* now entered the harbour, and went straight aground. She started disembarking her troops too. The volunteers jumped ashore with their arms at the ready; one of them was killed by a cannon-ball from the advancing Neapolitan men-of-war. Fishermen and local sailors and Neapolitan soldiers took to their heels. When a second cannon-ball landed, the English launch went rapidly up to the first Neapolitan cruiser, and immediately firing ceased. The bombardment was reopened only after the English launch returned to the corvette. By then it did not matter: Garibaldi was already ashore, and within two hours the Thousand were on Sicilian soil.

They entered the town, the garrison surrendered, and so did the governor. Windows and doors were closed, but some shops remained open, and the volunteers thronged them in search of food and drink. Before the arrival of the expedition the Marsala telegraphist had telegraphed to Trapani that two unknown ships were approaching the harbour. Then the telegraphist disappeared. Garibaldi, who was, as we know, an expert with telegrams, ordered his men to find another telegraphist. They found one at once. Garibaldi sent a telegram to Trapani in the name of the vanished telegraphist saying it was a false alarm, the ships in question were carrying English recruits to Malta. Trapani replied calling the telegraphist an imbecile for his mistake.

When evening came Garibaldi sent his advance guard towards Calatafimi. The rest of the army was to leave in the morning for Rambingallo. The night was noisy in Marsala, a few windows were timidly opened, and a timid "Viva Garibaldi!" was heard a few times by the troops. Not a word, remarks the French eyewitness H. Durand-Brager, about showers of flowers for the Garibaldians, as later recounted, was true. The good people of Marsala were too much afraid of Maniscalco, the head of the Sicilian police, and his sbirri. At three o'clock in the morning the Garibaldians began assembling, and by four they marched out of Marsala with Bixio, Orsini, Türr and Carini at their head. The artillery consisted of three pieces, ammunition was not abundant, and the guides had among them about a dozen horses. This was the army that would conquer Sicily and defeat the Neapolitans, who, as it will be seen, did their best to make the conquest possible.

Durand-Brager, who was a painter and had met Garibaldi in South America, certainly made one mistake when describing the landing in Marsala. There was not one English warship: there were two, and it was due to their presence that the Neapolitan cruisers could not blow the *Piedmonte* and the *Lombardo* out of the sea and destroy the expedition. They were the *Intrepid* and the *Argus* belonging to the Mediterranean Squadron commanded by Rear-Admiral Sir Rodney Mundy, K.C.B.

He had sailed from Malta with four sail of the line on 5th May to cruise off the east coast of Sicily, and on the 6th he had the good fortune of saving the life of a seaman by throwing his ring lifebuoy into the arms of the struggler; in his memoirs he strongly recommends every officer in command of a ship who has a stern cabin to have such a life-preserver at hand. His flagship was H.M.S. *Hannibal*. On 15th May he returned to port and heard that Garibaldi had landed at Marsala with twelve hundred men. The commander-in-chief, Vice-Admiral Arthur Fanshawe, ordered Admiral Mundy to proceed in the *Hannibal*, bearing his flag, to Palermo to provide additional means of protection to British persons and property, and he would take under his orders the *Amphion*, *Argus* and *Intrepid*. He should caution his officers and men to avoid taking part in any political discussions or disturbances.

Now came the tricky point of political refugees, who might, of course, have included Garibaldi and his Thousand if they had been defeated. H. W. Addington wrote to the Secretary of the Admiralty:

> Viscount Palmerston directs me to request that you will acquaint the Board of Admiralty that his Lordship is of opinion that it would not be right to receive and harbour on board a British ship of war any person flying from justice on a criminal charge or who was escaping from the sentence of a Court of Law. But a British ship of war has always and everywhere been considered a safe place of refuge for persons of whatever country or party who have sought shelter under the British flag from persecution on account of their political conduct or opinions, and the protection has been equally afforded whether the refugee was escaping from the arbitrary acts of a monarchical government, or from the lawless violence of a revolutionary committee.

Lord Palmerston saw no reason why a British ship of war stationed in a Neapolitan or Sicilian port should make an exception to the general rule. He saw also no reason "why the fact of a British officer having exercised this act of usual hospitality should entitle the Government of the country to order him out of the port, if the interests of

Her Majesty's service should require that he should remain there".

In short the Royal Navy could have played the part of Switzerland in the Como campaign during the Sicilian invasion. Admiral Mundy steamed into the bay of Palermo on 20th May. There he found both the *Amphion* and the *Intrepid*; France was represented by the paddle steam frigate *Vauban*; and Turin by two small steamers of war. Palermo was already in a state of siege. On the following day at 8 a.m. the *Hannibal* fired a royal salute, hoisting the Neapolitan flag. It was returned by the guns of the citadel. At 11 a.m. Admiral Mundy proceeded to the palace to pay an official visit to General Lanza, the *alter ego* of Francis II. The admiral found the town, which he surveyed from an open landau, deserted as if the plague were about. Not a vehicle, not an inhabitant was to be seen; but troops were everywhere. During his call on General Lanza no mention was made of political matters, that is of the island having been invaded. Nevertheless the admiral addressed a letter on his return to the *Hannibal* conveying his regrets that Marshal Salzano had informed the British Consul that he would not be able to afford any protection to British persons and property in the event of an insurrection in Palermo. It being currently reported that in the event of an insurrection a bombardment of the city by the forts and Neapolitan ships was in contemplation, Admiral Mundy asked to be given ample notice in order that, if possible, the property of British subjects might be saved from destruction. He added: "I trust, however, that a measure so extreme and deplorable as the bombardment of an open town may not be resorted to."

Garibaldi marched out of Marsala on the 12th, but before leaving he sent a message to Commander Ingram of the *Argus*, requesting him to take under his protection the sailors of the *Piedmonte* and the *Lombardo*. The request was turned down by the commander, and his admiral fully agreed with him; for it was, as he put it, most important at a moment of lawless invasion to abstain from an interference certain of misconstruction.

That takes us to an interesting point. Whether the vice-consul of Messina was Levantine or not, whether Mme Schwartz disliked him or not, he did put in a nutshell Her Britannic Majesty's Government's attitude; therefore Garibaldi was, for once, politically clever when, against the advice and influence of the Mazzinians, he invaded the island with the cry of "Italy and Victor Emmanuel!" and declared himself Dictator of Sicily in the name of Victor Emmanuel. One should not forget, however, that he liked the king and disliked Mazzini.

Garibaldi's first serious encounter with the Neapolitans was at Calatafimi. All the advantages were on the Neapolitan side. They were posted on high ground, and were about four thousand strong. Garibaldi's own force consisted of the men who landed from the two steamers, six hundred who had joined him from Castel Vitrano, seven hundred from Trapani, and three hundred who came with him from Marsala. He advanced from the town of Salemi, placed the Thousand on the right flank of the Neapolitans, Coppola with the men from Trapani on the left, and the rest in front.

The Neapolitans started the battle with an attack on the Thousand who fell pretending they were killed, though in reality they crawled forward on their bellies. When they got close enough they jumped to their feet, discharged a volley, then charged with the bayonet. On the other side Coppola and his men gained the summit too, and between them they drove the Neapolitans down the hill. The Neapolitans took up another position, but were driven

from it. Then they reversed their muskets, putting the
muzzles into the ground, and wanted to surrender. Their
commander, General Laudi, shamed them out of it. But
the battle was lost to them, and next day they fell back on
Alcamo. Garibaldi hurried through Calatafimi in pursuit
of them.

The fleeing Neapolitans burnt down forty houses in
Alcamo, murdered women and children, and started
pillaging. The inhabitants rose, killing thirty soldiers.
Garibaldi entered Alcamo on the 18th, and took possession
of it in the name of Victor Emmanuel. The road to
Palermo was practically open. When our French observer
reached Alcamo he saw the corpses of the Neapolitan
soldiers in a field, taken there by the inhabitants for dogs
and birds to feast on them. Sentries had been posted in
order to keep away any charitable soul who might wish
to bury them. But when Garibaldi arrived he ordered their
burial at once.

It was in Alcamo that the insurrection began to take
shape on a big scale. With his victory at Calatafimi and
with the Neapolitans holding back in great irresolution
and without initiative, the Sicilians perceived that this at
last was serious, therefore risks could be taken.

There was nothing irresolute about Garibaldi. The one
chance in a hundred had come off: now he pushed forward
as fast as he could. He marched on Piappo, then the
picciotti, the peasant-volunteers of Sicily, came on the
Neapolitans' rear a few miles from San Martino. The
Neapolitans first pushed back the picciotti and killed their
colonel, Roselino Pilo, but the picciotti counter-attacked,
and the Neapolitans withdrew. That was on 21st May.

In pouring rain Garibaldi took the road from Rena to
Parco. On the 24th, at Parco, Garibaldi saw deep columns
of Neapolitan soldiers advancing towards him, and other

Neapolitan columns from Montreale began to threaten his left flank. He ordered the left flank to hold out till the last man. His small artillery swept the columns both from Palermo and Montreale. Rapidly his centre and the right flank reached Piano dei Greci. The Neapolitans, in fear of being outflanked, retreated in their terror. La Masa's squadre (peasant contingents) had taken to their heels the day before, for they thought that Garibaldi was retreating into the interior. La Masa, however, rallied at Gibilrossa, and wrote to Garibaldi to join him, and then to attack Palermo together. When night came Garibaldi did one of his vanishing acts. They crossed the plain by the Corleone high road, and when they were, with artillery and all, two miles from Corleone they left the road, and aided by darkness, his military ally, they reached the village of Santa Cristina Gela, then took a rough road to the east. The troops rested for a while in a wood. Next day they reached Marineo, but did not stay, for Garibaldi ordered them on to Misilmeri, and a messenger was sent to La Masa at Gibilrossa that he would see him at three in the morning on the following day in order to make important arrangements. The arrangements meant onslaught on Palermo.

During their long march, with the Neapolitans never quite catching up with them, the inhabitants of villages and hamlets stayed behind barred windows and doors. They still feared the brutality of the Neapolitans. But there was no traitor among them, and no intelligence reached the Neapolitans about the movements of the Thousand.

II

On 26th May Admiral Mundy was informed by General Lanza, the *alter ego*, that the rebels had been driven into the mountains, so the admiral thought he would take a drive in an open carriage in the afternoon. On the out-skirts of the city he gained admission into a mansion once occupied by the Moorish governors of Sicily, and looking out on the richly cultivated plain he saw only smoke of ruins and devastation. There was continuous firing on the slopes of the hills. On his way back to the Mole he saw a number of men handcuffed under the escort of sbirri, Maniscalco's policemen. The men were searched, only a few hard biscuits and a little tobacco was found on them. They had been visiting the English ships of war. They were thrown into prison. "Verily," remarks the admiral, "acts such as these, in violation of the first principles of justice, and tending to exasperate a class of community which it should have been the effort of the ruling power to conciliate, are beyond comprehension."

An English gentleman, who had remained in his house in the city and did not follow his compatriots to the battleships, sent a note to the admiral informing him that the rising in Palermo would take place at two on the following morning, and Garibaldi would be near the Porta Sant' Antonio, ready to force his way into the city with the bayonet. Apparently everybody knew of it except the Neapolitans.

Two young naval officers, Lieutenants Wilmot and Cooper, and Mr Morgan, paymaster, made an excursion on the previous day to the village of Misilmeri, and immense was their surprise when they heard that Garibaldi was at dinner in a neighbouring vineyard. When Garibaldi heard that English naval officers were driving through the village, he sent a messenger to take them to his head-quarters. They found him in the middle of a large enclosure surrounded by about twenty followers in grey trousers and red flannel shirts. Garibaldi was dressed in the same fashion. Menotti, stout and tall, was with his father. Garibaldi bade the Englishmen sit down, offered them fresh strawberries, and spoke of the beautiful effect produced by the royal salutes of the ships of war in honour of Queen Victoria's birthday. He had heard and seen it from Piano dei Greci. He also expressed his hope to meet the English admiral on his arrival in Palermo; and the English admiral, when he heard of the excursion, issued an order to his officers with reference to the armed bands under General Garibaldi that until further orders no officer should go beyond the limits of the sentinels of the royal troops.

On Whitsunday, 27th May, Admiral Mundy was wakened by firing. He saw Neapolitan troops retreating at the double from the guardhouse at the eastern end of the Marina towards the gate of the citadel. They had hardly passed the entrance to the Toledo when a party of insurgents with tricolour flags rushed after the royal troops, advancing boldly on the citadel hoping to prevent their escape. The citadel opened fire. The rebels fell back, and then from the shelter of the houses started to build barricades. Shortly after six o'clock the Neapolitan squadron began to bombard the town indiscriminately. The bombardment ceased at eight o'clock. By then Garibaldi had established his headquarters in the Piazza del Pretorio— the right man in the right place, by which we mean that he stood in the right spot under the apple tree to catch and squash the falling rotten apple.

At 3 p.m. the bombardment of Palermo began again. The answer was the ringing of the bells of churches and convents. Shortly before sunset Marshal Salzano was seen descending from Montreale with his troops. At its foot they were stopped by the squadre, preventing their junction with the main body of the Neapolitans. The town was burning. By midnight the bells stopped ringing and the bombardment ceased.

At daybreak on the 28th the political prisoners escaped from the western suburbs of the city, attacked the troops, and captured the outlying barracks. The Neapolitan gunboats played on the insurgents and heavy guns shelled the Pretorio. Captain Cossovich, in command of his Sicilian Majesty's *Parthenope*, came to the *Hannibal* requesting an interview with Admiral Mundy. It was to be most confidential and secret. Admiral Mundy told him to speak deliberately and to make known his mission.

Captain Cossovich informed him that all communication between Royal headquarters and the fleet was cut off by the insurgents, messages could be received only by semaphores, and he had received a telegraphic cipher from General Lanza to ask the English admiral whether an English merchant ship had brought despatches from his government, and if so would he forward them to the Palace.

That interview was the first tentative approach by the Neapolitans for negotiations, which were protracted but ended in Garibaldi and the Neapolitan generals Letizia and Chrétien meeting in the *Hannibal* at 2.15 p.m. on 30th May.

When General Letizia and General Chrétien had seated themselves in the boat to go on board the *Hannibal* they were flabbergasted as Garibaldi stepped calmly in and sat down at their side. They had not seen him before, and had not noticed his bodyguard when they drove down in state in the viceregal barouche, with its blue and scarlet liveries and attendant outriders. Now the *diavolo* was in the boat with them, and they were much embittered. "Out boat-hooks", came the order, and "Shove off", and beside Garibaldi the poor generals had to remain till they reached the flagship.

Garibaldi was the first to step on the quarter-deck. The Royal generals had insisted on his going first. Garibaldi wore the uniform of a Sardinian general and was saluted by the guard of Marine Light Infantry according to his rank. The same honours were paid to the two Neapolitans. The captains of the French, American and Sardinian ships of war, whom Admiral Mundy had invited for the conference, accompanied them into his cabin. General Letizia, who had been boiling up in the boat, gruffly exclaimed that he would not enter into communication with the admiral in the presence of the captains of other nations. Nor was he willing to recognize Garibaldi in any official capacity or to confer with him. All mediations must take place between the British admiral, himself and his colleague. Those were the instructions he had received from the *alter ego*, General Lanza.

The British admiral did not care for his dictatorial tone. He asked Garibaldi if he felt the same objection to the presence of the captains in command of the squadrons of three friendly Powers. Garibaldi answered that any arrangement Mundy thought fit to make would be perfectly agreeable to him. General Letizia repeated his objections in even stronger terms. Captain Lefèvre of the French steam frigate *Vauban* expressed with great precision in his native tongue his astonishment at the conduct and language of General Letizia. He was seconded by Captain Palmer of the U.S. frigate *Iroquois*, who, since he could speak neither French nor Italian, was unable to give the same force to his expressions. The Sardinian captain, Marchese d'Asti, remained silent; Garibaldi, unperturbed.

The altercation became so unseemly and noisy that Admiral Mundy told General Letizia that he was utterly unable to understand the meaning of his violent conduct, and if he continued to refuse to treat with Garibaldi, and

in the presence of the captains, he would be obliged to put
him ashore and declare the negotiations at an end. General
Letizia subsided into a calmer frame of mind, and after a
little while accepted the terms Admiral Mundy proposed.
Then the admiral made it clear to the two Neapolitans
"that from the moment they trod on the deck of the
Hannibal and so came under the protection of the British
flag, they met together on terms of perfect equality", and
Garibaldi was entitled to the same courtesy and respect as
generals of the Royal army. The three generals sat down
at a small round table.

General Letizia produced a paper containing six articles.
Then speaking of himself in the third person he said he was
a very old officer, had fought many bloody campaigns,
therefore he thought very little of the present aspect of
affairs in Palermo, but he would be glad for the sake of
humanity if hostilities were suspended. Garibaldi sarcastically congratulated him and General Chrétien on their good
fortune; he himself could not flatter himself on having had
equal experience, especially as he had acted only once in
his life with a regular army. Then he asked to see the six
articles. The first four were agreed to. They contained
suspension of arms, the evacuation of the wounded from
the Royal Palace to the Royal ships, and the troops in the
Palace and the Royalist refugees in the monasteries should
be allowed to provide themselves with their daily provisions. But then came the fifth article: "That the municipality should address a humble petition to His Majesty
the King [Francis II] laying before him the real wishes of
the town, and that this petition should be submitted to His
Majesty."

"No!" shouted Garibaldi vehemently. He drew himself
up. "The time for humble petitions, either to the king or to
any other person, is past. Besides, there is no longer any

The Siege of Gaeta: dead Piedmontese after the unsuccessful
attempt to storm the citadel, 1861

The Fortress of Verona during the Revolution of 1848

Garibaldi on his white charger,
wearing his poncho

municipality. *La municipalité, c'est moi!* I refuse my assent. Pass on to the sixth and last provision."

"Then, sir," said General Letizia, folding up the paper, "unless the article is agreed to, all communications between us must cease."

It was Garibaldi's turn to use vehement language. He lost his temper completely as he shouted at the Royal generals. They lacked good faith, were infamous and treacherous. (Some of the newly landed Royal troops had not respected the cease-fire.) Perfidy was another word he used. General Letizia became equally eloquent—and you can almost see Admiral Mundy's expression. General Letizia appealed to him, saying there could surely be nothing derogatory in a petition which should be humbly laid at His Majesty's feet. The admiral reminded him that he was not acting as mediator, he simply offered, in strict neutrality, an opportunity for each contracting party to settle their differences, and he could not offer any opinion. General Letizia then asked what could be the object of the presence of foreign captains if it was not to give advice. Captain Lefèvre demolished in a masterly exposition the fabric of objections. He too was disgusted with the violent language.

Garibaldi thought that the negotiations were broken off, so rose from the table. The two Neapolitans quickly consulted among themselves, as a result of which they agreed to expunge the fifth article, and moved on to the sixth, which concerned feeding the Royal troops in the town. Garibaldi accepted that. The armistice was agreed to till noon on the following day. The Neapolitans asked the admiral to speak to them in private. They apologized for the Bavarian contingent having advanced on the insurgents after the truce, and expressed their hope that Garibaldi, who had shown such readiness to accept their proposals, would agree to a prolongation of the armistice till the Royal generals went to and returned from Naples. Garibaldi did not speak to the admiral in private, but on re-landing at the Porta Felice he accepted General Letizia's invitation to ride with them in the viceregal barouche. They dropped him in the nearest street leading to the Pretorio. In the Piazza dei Quatro Cantoni Garibaldi made a speech to the populace, which, says the admiral, "though well adapted to the fervid imagination of the Italian people, sounds bombastic and puerile in the ears of the more sedate Northmen". With the word "puerile" both Cavour and Mazzini would have agreed, though neither of them was a Northman.

<h1 style="text-align:center">III</h1>

General Letizia returned from Naples on 6th June. The armistice had been extended. A convention had been signed between General Lanza and Francesco Crispi, whom Garibaldi had appointed as Secretary of State for the Provisional Government, and as a result of the convention the Royal Mint was handed over to Garibaldi. The squadre had been promoted to Cacciatori dell' Etna, and now received their first pay. General Letizia brought with him full powers to treat with Garibaldi, and a new convention was signed whereby the Royal troops would evacuate Palermo with arms, baggage and material, and with all the honours of war.

About twelve thousand Neapolitan troops were marched into the citadel, their march taking them past, and having at times to zigzag among the mounted barricades of the Garibaldians. Transports arrived from Naples. The sick and the wounded went first, followed by baggage and troops, the soldiers looking far from depressed, with their bands playing, and giving the general impression of conquerors embarking on some new adventure. They left behind three hundred burnt-down houses in the quarter of Albergheria alone.

After the departure of the Neapolitans, reinforcements began to arrive by sea for Garibaldi. When the ships *Utile* and *Charles and Jane* appeared with new batches of volunteers brought from Genoa by Medici, the Dictator immediately mounted his horse to receive them appropriately. When night fell on that day, which was 11th June, and the vivas, cheering and music died away, and dark midnight came into its own, the good people of Palermo were suddenly frightened by the sound of cannon out at sea. Windows opened, women trembled, children cried, and patrols were alerted in the streets. In the barracks soldiers were called to arms; could it be the Neapolitans coming back? The cannonade grew in volume. Everybody rushed to the port, troops came marching in the same direction. Everybody bemoaned that the Dictator was away at Castellamare; here they were leaderless and any minute now the poor town would be bombarded again. The picciotti were becoming restless, wanted to attack, though there was no sign yet of anybody who ought to be attacked, then out of the blue, or rather the darkness, appeared a boat of the Royal Navy, a midshipman came ashore to inform the authorities that an English ship of war was out on gunnery practice. Does not that, asks Durand-Brager, who was in the frightened crowd, show what the English are like?

A strong Sardinian squadron reached Palermo on the 9th July. With Garibaldi successful, the king and Cavour were coming into the open. The presence of the squadron was of great moral help for the Dictator insofar as it quietened those who wanted neither revolution nor republic. La Farina came with the squadron bringing a message from Cavour that Sicily should immediately be annexed to the constitutional kingdom of Victor Emmanuel. Garibaldi refused to consider annexation before the entire island was freed from the Neapolitans, and to prove that he was not joking he sent La Farina packing. Garibaldi had moved into the Royal Palace. The viceregal servants were astonished by the Dictator's simple habits. His meals consisted of soup and vegetables, meat only once a day, and his wardrobe consisted of . . . never mind, we know that it consisted of very little. But he did go to the *Te Deum* at the cathedral, and knelt among the crowd. When he chased La Farina off the island he was not thinking only of the complete conquest of Sicily: Naples and of course Rome were his real objectives.

With the reinforcements Medici brought, and with the respectability the presence of Admiral Persano's squadron gave him in the eyes of the Constitutionalists, he decided to push on. General Türr was sent through the centre of the island, Bixio moved along the south coast, and Medici took the northern road towards Messina, which, after Palermo, was the most important target.

In Palermo a number of brutal murders were committed, and on the pretext of revenging themselves on the sbirri, innocent people were knifed to death by private enemies. One evening in the Toledo, a poor fellow was chased by the mob. He tried to find refuge in a pharmacy, but the chemist banged the door in his face, and he was massacred on the spot, and if passers-by, including women, saw a corpse in the street, they kicked it, observing that it was probably the corpse of a sbirro. A corps of Sicilian volunteers entered the town. Their commander, an ardent young man of good family, having dined with his family, was returning to his corps when one of his volunteers stopped him to ask for money, which he refused, and he was immediately killed by the man. Eventually the man was caught and executed in the Piazza della Bagheria.

On 20th June, with the English ships of war dressed with flags in honour of the anniversary of Queen Victoria's accession to the throne, a Royal salute was fired by all ships in port; and Garibaldi, without knowing anything about it, chose that day to pay a call on the foreign ships in port. The *Racoon*, the *Scylla* and the *Caradoc* had joined the English squadron, which was anchored nearer to the quay than any of the others. Admiral Mundy thought it was possible that the Dictator, as he embarked in the barge of the Sardinian ship of war *Maria Adelaide*, was not averse to the thought that the salute had been fired in his honour. That misconception had certainly gained the lower orders in Palermo.

The *Maria Adelaide* gave Garibaldi the salute of nineteen guns due to a viceroy. Mundy found that a bold measure. From the Sardinian ship of war the Dictator came to the *Hannibal*, wearing red shirt and grey trousers. He had improved his appearance by putting on his head a Tyrolean hat with black plumes. The admiral thought that he felt more at home in that apparel than in a general's uniform. He also observed the narrow waist and broad hips of the Dictator.

The admiral received him on the quarter-deck. Though he was given the same military honours as on his previous visit, the admiral made it clear to him that he could not recognize him as Dictator, nor could he salute him on his departure as the head of the provisional government of Palermo. Garibaldi assured him that he neither wished nor expected to be received in an official capacity. He had come to thank the admiral for having stopped the bombardment and for having brought about the armistice. He said his

gratitude would be eternal, and eternal too was his love
for England and the British people. Then Garibaldi spoke
with satisfaction of the English squadron having anchored
so close to the shore. The admiral said he did that because
of the exceptional circumstances. He did not mention,
however, that during the hostilities he had kept the
Intrepid only at a stone's throw from the Marina, and that
he had "placed that well disciplined little craft, commanded by Captain Marryat, off the nearest rocks close
to the Toledo for the purpose of saving Garibaldi's own
life should a stroke of adverse fortune compel him to
look around for an ark of safety".

From the *Hannibal* Garibaldi went to the French flagship,
and in the afternoon Rear-Admiral Jehenne came to see
Mundy to tell him that the Dictator's visit had placed him
in an untoward position, and he was obliged to tell his
visitor that he could not receive him even as a general
officer, but only as plain monsieur.

The Dictator took to confiscating the property of
religious Orders; he was made an honorary citizen of
Palermo; and at the same time the municipal council made
it very clear to him that they wanted annexation by Victor
Emmanuel. "I came to fight for Italy," he told them, "and
not for Sicily alone, and until Italy is entirely liberated I
shall do nothing for one party or another." The councillors
were not pleased with the reply, and posters appeared
all over the town clamouring for annexation by Victor
Emmanuel. A poster appeared too, signed by a distinguished
local lawyer, exhorting the people to follow the worthy
example of their ancestors and start another Sicilian Ves-
pers.

Dumas arrived in Palermo in his yacht. The Dictator
put him up in the State Apartments. Shortly after Dumas
set out for the front, accompanied by two pointers and a

female dressed as a midshipman. The great gastronomer changed his mind halfway and returned to the comparative ease of Palermo.

Garibaldi was spending money, and the good Palermitans did not approve of their money being spent in buying ships and ammunition; nor did they care for their church-bells being turned into cannon. Moreover, they were tiring of dressing up Bourbon statues with ox-heads, and, needless to add since we are in the Mediterranean, with horns. They got bored too with kicking those statues about.

On 17th July Garibaldi, who proved to be a bad organizer, was relieved of that obnoxious task by a telegram Medici sent him. The Neapolitans, based on Messina, which it was believed they would defend energetically, were concentrating large forces near Milazzo. Milazzo was to be Garibaldi's most resounding victory.

He sailed on 17th July on board the *City of Aberdeen*. There were shouts of "Viva Garibaldi!" but coupled with "Viva Vittorio Emmanuele!" by the sailors of the Piedmontese squadron, under the command of Admiral Count Persano, as the *City of Aberdeen* sailed past. If that squadron had not been in Sicilian waters, one wonders whether the Neapolitans, in spite of their lack of energy and impetus, would not have sent their warships back and made things damnably difficult for the Dictator. Some observers believed that without Admiral Persano's squadron the Dictator's position would have become untenable; and there could have been no victory of Milazzo if Cavour had not allowed the reinforcements through, or if he had not been using all his diplomatic skill to appease the French Emperor. On the other hand, without Garibaldi's audacity there could have been no successful Sicilian campaign, in fact no campaign at all.

General Bosco of the Neapolitan army was a general who believed in fighting. At Milazzo he even had the intention of defeating Garibaldi. The Neapolitan commander-in-chief, General Clary, remained in Messina, in the almost impregnable citadel. Messina was now practically cut off from the rest of the island, only the postal service functioned with more or less regularity, and through the post arrived the texts of Garibaldi's edicts and proclamations in Palermo for all Sicilians; and when an order from the Dictator arrived by post ordering all civil servants and magistrates to leave for Barcellona, it was stuck up on the walls and immediately obeyed, the sole exception being the director of the bank. On 14th July several transports arrived bringing Garibaldian volunteers from Calabria. The volunteers disembarked unmolested only a mile and a half from Messina, then took to the Taormina road. They were not interfered with.

General Bosco left Messina on the same day with three columns at 3 a.m. The first column marched beside the sea in order to join up with the garrison of Milazzo; the second column in the centre; the third towards the mountains. General Bosco's army consisted of four battalions of chasseurs, several squadrons of mounted chasseurs and lancers, and two batteries. The advance guard of the Garibaldians withdrew in front of the Neapolitans to Linieri and Meri, two small towns three miles distant from Barcellona.

While Medici's troops withdrew, General Fabrizi moved through the mountains so as to cut off General Bosco from Messina. Garibaldi's army was by now a motley gathering, which included an English brigade under Colonel Dunne, but the troops were mostly Sicilians; then there were French and Hungarian contingents, also Colonel Peard's revolving-rifle company. Colonel Peard was usually known as Garibaldi's Englishman. Colonel Peard during the battle pushed on to the town of Milazzo, which lay at the foot of the castle, but was soon brought to a standstill by Bosco's men.

On 17th July Medici informed Garibaldi, who was still in Palermo, that the enemy had tried to turn his right, but was repulsed. Later in the day he sent a second dispatch: the enemy attacked again, but was repulsed after two hours of hard fighting and two bayonet charges. The enemy withdrew on Milazzo.

The town of Milazzo is situated at the entrance of a narrow isthmus. Above the town stood the castle on a hill. The town was surrounded by vineyards. After the encounters with Medici the Neapolitans took up their position on the main road and its surroundings, their artillery being on the road itself in front of a bridge. Medici's army was on the plain in front of Barcellona, though separated from the Royal troops only by two miles. On the 20th battle was joined, the first to fall on the enemy were Colonel Dunne's Anglo-Sicilians. The Neapolitans were far superior in artillery; moreover, the fighting took place on their ground. There had, however, already been a mutiny in the castle among Neapolitans.

The Garibaldians were pushed back; the Neapolitan fire was steady and effective; the volunteers were badly mauled; then, suddenly, the rumour spread from mouth to mouth: "Garibaldi is here!"

A fresh Piedmontese regiment was sent forward, and before the attack began Garibaldi put himself at its head. The rest of the army followed. The Neapolitans were forced off the road at the point of the bayonet, but every vineyard had to be fought for. The withdrawing enemy left a cannon on the road; about ten lancers were sent back to fetch it; and they passed Garibaldi, who was with Missori, Statella and some of Dunne's men, without noticing him. On their return, without the cannon of course, they caught sight of the Dictator and the small group round him, and charged. Garibaldi with his sabre nearly cut off the arm of the Neapolitan major in command of the troop. Missori killed two, and eventually the lancers made off, leaving behind eight of their comrades dead. Hence only two got away. (There are several versions of this encounter, some deny Garibaldi fighting anybody. The above version is taken from the eyewitness Durand-Brager, who adds: "Hang thyself, Dumas, for not having been present to tell of this battle worthy of d'Artagnan!")

After the brief engagement Garibaldi took his shirt off, washed it in a brook, hung it on a bush, ate his lunch, lit a cigar, waited till his shirt was dry, put it on, then threw his troops against the isthmus, and afraid of being outflanked the Neapolitans beat a hasty retreat to the castle. The Garibaldians came hot on their heels, chasing them through the town, which fell to them. Meanwhile the *Veloce*, a Neapolitan ship of war that had joined Garibaldi, shelled the castle. That stopped General Bosco from making a sortie. By then it was 5.30 p.m.

The Royal troops were now locked up in the castle. Those who had not succeeded in getting into the castle, were running for dear life towards Messina. The Garibaldians lost about eight hundred men, the Neapolitans three hundred.

The 21st and 22nd July were spent by the Garibaldians in laying siege to the castle. On the 23rd in the morning three French ships appeared, chartered by the Neapolitans, bringing munitions and provisions for the Royal troops. Big was the surprise of the first French captain, M. de

Salvi, when he was taken to Garibaldi. He had, naturally, expected to see General Bosco. A French warship, the *Mouette*, arrived, and the commander ordered the cargo vessels to make for Messina. But M. de Salvi, who had brought an urgent message from Naples for General Bosco, asked Garibaldi to permit him to go up to the castle. Permission was given, and he asked M. de Salvi to acquaint the Royal general with his own conditions for surrender. Officers could go free; the men, however, would be taken prisoners. M. de Salvi reached the castle and saw General Bosco. The general declared he would surrender under no circumstances whatever, he would rather die at the head of his troops than hoist the white flag. M. de Salvi rejoined Garibaldi, who gave him new conditions; he saw Bosco again, who this time said he did not want to sacrifice human lives either, but it was a matter of honour.

Leaving the castle M. de Salvi caught sight of four Neapolitan frigates approaching. He hurried to his ship, afraid for her safety in case the frigates opened fire on the Garibaldians. There was no need for fear. The frigates brought a Royal colonel from Naples to arrange the capitulation of General Bosco's army. On the 24th the troops—there were more than four thousand—began to embark on the French ships, which had been called back from Messina, and on the 25th the Garibaldians occupied the castle. General Bosco had deserved better from his king. The inhabitants of Milazzo had vanished before the battle began; not one of them came to volunteer for Garibaldi, but with equal impartiality they gave no help to the Neapolitans either.

Dumas, who was miles and miles away, tells us that the night after the battle of Milazzo he found Garibaldi in the town, spending the night on the porch of a church, his head on a saddle, a jug of water and a loaf at his side. As a matter of fact Garibaldi passed the night in a comfortable bed in the English consul's house. The road to Messina was not only open, but already thronged with Garibaldians, and the Neapolitans began to evacuate their troops to the mainland, leaving behind only garrisons for the forts. Medici was sent to Messina, and came to terms with General Clary. The forts of Gonzaga and San Salvatore were to be handed over to Garibaldi: the citadel was retained by the Neapolitans. The town and harbour of Messina would not be bombarded by the Neapolitans if the Garibaldians kept to the arrangement.

The inhabitants of Messina, that is those who could afford it, evacuated themselves to sea, filling merchant ships, small vessels and even boats. Anything up to fifteen francs was charged for a seat in a boat. Garibaldi arrived and was received with waving tricolours. On 30th July the Neapolitan troops were evacuated by sea, only the garrison of the citadel remained, shops and cafés opened again, and the good people returned from the sea. Soon Dumas made his entry into Messina, and strolling in the now fervent city Durand-Brager heard the crowd shouting: "Viva Italia! Viva Garibaldi! Viva la libertà! Viva Dumas! Viva Vittorio Emmanuele!"

The next move would be to cross the Straits of Messina, and preparations for the invasion of the mainland began in a big way. Francis II in Naples remembered Victor Emmanuel's letter, and sent plenipotentiaries to Turin. They were entertained lavishly, and Victor Emmanuel let them know that it was too late to stem the impetus of the nation, though he would do what he could. And truly enough he sent Garibaldi a letter ordering him not to cross the Straits. The letter was sent by Count Litta, who carried another letter to the Dictator, the intention of which was "to neutralize the effect of the first". In that letter the king told him to "reply that you are full of devotion and reverence for your King . . . but that your duty to Italy forbids you to promise not to help the Neapolitans when they appeal to you to free them from a Government which true men and good Italians cannot trust: that you cannot, therefore, obey the wishes of the King. . . ."

Garibaldi laughed when he read the second letter, and answered it at once saying he held the king in high esteem, loved him too, but the present state of things in Italy did not allow him to obey the king; called by the people he refrained as long as he could; now, however, he would fail in his duty if he delayed the calls for help that reached him; but as soon as he had fulfilled what he had undertaken he would lay down his sword at the king's feet and obey him for the rest of his life. As we shall see, he did not; on the other hand, could he be really blamed, with the example the king and Cavour set? Should he be a rebel only when it suited others?

Another secret message reached Garibaldi, brought to him by the king's aide-de-camp Trecchi. The king ordered Garibaldi not only to occupy the capital of a kingdom he was not at war with, namely Naples, but to push on from Naples and invade Papal Territory, that is Umbria and the Marches. The king's intention was to keep Garibaldi quiet while Cavour was putting the finishing touches to his own plans, which, however, depended on Garibaldi getting to Naples, since Victor Emmanuel and Cavour would not themselves have yet dared, because of Napoleon III, to invade the Neapolitan Kingdom. The whole thing was masterly and as crooked as possible. From the moment that the king and Cavour heard of Garibaldi's successes in Sicily, they had decided on invading Papal Territory if Garibaldi reached Naples. Never for an instant did they want Garibaldi to enter the Papal States. But it was in their interest to make him think that he could and that they were in favour of it. Bertani from Genoa wanted to attack the Papal States. Cavour stopped that, for he did not want the Mazzinians to forestall him. Bertani was told by Farini in Cavour's name that the king's government intended to invade the Papal States before many days. The volunteers, under Pianciani, therefore would be sent out to Garibaldi. It was enough to cope with Garibaldi: Cavour needed no other leader, with volunteers and all. Dr Bertani had no intention of obeying, so he sailed to Sicily to persuade Garibaldi to come to the Golfo degli Aranci, meet his volunteers there (they had been given permission to sail from Genoa to Sardinia on their way to Garibaldi), then put himself at their head and lead them against the Papal States instead of taking them to Sicily. Garibaldi sailed with him to Sardinia on board the *Washington* on 12th August.

Garibaldi was in a sense at the crossroads. Naples or Rome? The matter was settled by Cavour, who did not fancy leaving decisions to the Dictator. When Garibaldi and Dr Bertani reached the Golfo degli Aranci they found only part of the volunteers and their fleet. Piedmontese ships of war had forced most of their vessels to continue to Sicily in accordance with Bertani's promise to the government. Thus Garibaldi was saved from making a choice. One feels that Bertani would have flattered him into an attack on the Papal States, which, without Piedmontese help, in fact against the plans of Piedmont, would certainly have miscarried.

He went to pass some hours in Caprera. By the time he arrived back in Sicily Pianciani's men had landed there. They were six thousand strong, and he badly needed reinforcements for attacking the mainland. After the occupation of Messina many of the Sicilians reached the conclusion that their war was over, and went home.

Two thousand more volunteers arrived in Sicily to strengthen Garibaldi's forces. They came from Tuscany, and under Nicotera formed part of Bertani's corps. They had been sent to Tuscany to invade the Papal States, but Baron Ricasoli, the Iron Baron of Tuscany, shipped them to Sicily too. Cavour's next move was to stop sending more reinforcements to Garibaldi, who, he thought, had enough men now to march on Naples. If he had more, there might easily be a diversion against the Papal States, which he had earmarked for himself, that is to the regular Piedmontese army because the king and his servant could implicitly trust it.

On 18th August Garibaldi crossed the Straits, and the military promenade to Naples began.

IV

In London it was felt too that Garibaldi needed volunteers. A committee was formed. The treasurer of the committee was George Jacob Holyoake, the secularist, who had had the distinction of being the last person in Britain convicted for blasphemy in a public lecture. That cost him six months' imprisonment. He had also the distinction of having brought together Kossuth, Ledru-Rollin and Mazzini for the purpose of a manifesto, which Holyoake's publishing house printed.

"A great movement must have an arm to raise the flag, a voice to cry aloud—*The hour has come!* We are that arm and that voice. . . . Advanced Guard of the Revolution, we shall disappear amid the ranks on the day of the awakening of the peoples. . . . We are not the future; we are its precursors. We are not the democracy; we are an army bound to clear the way for democracy."

"It was my intention," commented Holyoake, "to disappear in the ranks."

As treasurer of the Garibaldi Fund Committee he discovered that discord had its appointed place in matters of the Risorgimento. In one provincial town, for instance, a certain banker—Holyoake does not give his name—held four hundred pounds for the Fund, but was unwilling to pay it out to the Committee. Even De Rohan and W. H. Ashurst could not get it out of him. Holyoake travelled to the Midlands to see the banker, who, however, made himself unavailable on his approach, so he saw only his wife. Holyoake spoke to her, explained that the money was needed for and would be spent on Garibaldi's behalf, and the result of the visit was that eventually the banker sent him a cheque. Holyoake found out that the cause of the banker's unwillingness was his fear of the money falling into Mazzini's hands. The banker sympathized with Garibaldi's aims, which, what with "Viva Vittorio Emmanuele!" and support from the Piedmontese Navy sounded legitimate to him, but not with the word "revolution", which is not endearing to bankers.

Holyoake was equally devoted to Mazzini and Garibaldi, though Garibaldi would always forget his name. He saw a lot of Mazzini, whom he considered one of the finest men he had met. Therefore his anger was boundless when he heard that one morning a person purporting to be Mazzini called on Charles Dickens in Tavistock Place and solicited aid. Dickens sent down a servant, who presented the man with a sovereign on a silver tray. "How could he [Dickens] imagine," cried Holyoake, "that a gentleman whom he had met in society, as a man of reputation for honour and self-respect, would come to his door soliciting alms, like an adventurer or an impostor? And, if he believed the applicant to be Mazzini, some inquiry, some commisera-

Giuseppe
Mazzini

Count
Cavour

Garibaldi and members of the Workers' Union at a banquet given in his honour, 1875

Garibaldi was crippled with arthritis and his crutches are leaning against the chair of Venturi, Mayor of Rome. His eldest son, Menotti, is on the extreme left

tion and identification was necessary to make sure that one
so eminent was suddenly in distress so abject. Mazzini had
a hundred friends who would have aided him before he
need have been a suppliant at Dickens's door."

Anyway, there was the project of sending a British
Legion out to Garibaldi. Holyoake thought that the idea
came from De Rohan, an American, who had gathered
in Italy that British volunteers would influence Italian
opinion, and if sent out in time they might be of military
service. Soon the Garibaldi Fund Committee found itself
engaging volunteers. Holyoake was aware that among the
generous and the brave there would be some shady
creatures. However, he consoled himself, the army of
every country is largely recruited from the class of dubious
persons. The Committee took a house at 8 Salisbury
Street, Strand, London, which was turned into a recruiting
office. Among the volunteers appeared a young man,
calling himself Captain Styles, and wearing the uniform of
a Garibaldian soldier. Being early in the field and having
specious manners, the volunteers who came later took it
for granted that he had an official position, and it was
imagined that he had been in Italy and in some army.
His influence grew by not being questioned. Holyoake
apparently did not question him either, and found out
only afterwards that Captain Styles invented and secretly
sold commissions in the British Legion, putting the pro-
ceeds into his pocket. To avoid drawing attention to
their plan, the Committee drew up a notice after the
manner of Dr Lunn's tourist agency.

EXCURSION to SICILY and NAPLES. – All persons
(particularly Members of Volunteer Rifle Corps) desirous
of visiting Southern Italy, and of AIDING by their presence
and influence the CAUSE of GARIBALDI and ITALY,
may learn how to proceed by applying to the Garibaldi

Committee, at the offices at No. 8 Salisbury Street, Strand, London.

The excursionists received notice of two things. First: Each man should remember that he goes out to represent the sacred cause of Liberty, and the cause will be judged by his conduct. His behaviour will be as important as his bravery. Second: Those in command will respect the high feelings by which the humblest man is animated—but no man must make his equal patriotism a pretext for refusing implicit obedience to orders upon which his safety and usefulness depend.

About a thousand names were entered on the roll of volunteers. Now they had to be got out of the country, and, admits Holyoake, international law was not on their side. When the volunteers were ready to set out for Harwich on the Great Eastern Railway, Styles, who had promoted himself from captain to major, sent each of them a confidential note requesting their attendance at Caldwell's Assembly Rooms in Dean Street at 3 p.m. Captain de Rohan was put in command of the excursionists. In his new capacity he styled himself Rear-Admiral de Rohan, but he was an honest fellow. He travelled in advance of the Legion, and was waiting for them in Palermo when they arrived. Major Styles vanished and no more was heard of him. As the Legion arrived too late for the Sicilian campaign, it was sent on to Naples. Admiral Mundy, who was in the Bay of Naples with his squadron, saw them arrive. That was already after the battle of the Volturno.

"In the afternoon," wrote the admiral on 14th October, "two English steamers arrived bringing the British Volunteer Legion, numbering about six hundred men. They were all dressed in scarlet uniform and looked remarkably well. Unfortunately there is no longer probability of active work in the field for these hardy sons of Albion."

And Garibaldi wrote after his return to Caprera: "They came late. But they made ample amends for this defect, not their own, by the brilliant courage they displayed in the slight engagement they shared with us near the Volturno. . . . In every way the English volunteers were a proof of the goodwill borne by your noble nation towards the liberty and independence of Italy."

But perhaps Cavour was the man whom the excursionists remembered most; for when they were repatriated he gave orders that they were to be supplied with double rations, as, he said, Englishmen ate more than Italians.

Garibaldi did not take long in arriving in Naples. Very little resistance was offered him. General Briganti of the Neapolitan Army was murdered in Mileto by Neapolitan troops. The general had tried to retreat privately, dressed as a civilian. The soldiers fell on him, emptied their rifles into him, then mutilated his body and burnt his horse in the presence of Neapolitan officers, who did not dare to interfere. Some of the soldiers said they killed him because he was a Liberal and a traitor, others because they wanted his boots.

During that military promenade Garibaldi remained mostly with General Türr's division. On 4th September, coming from Monte Cucuzzo, Garibaldi rested at an inn in Il Fortino. In that inn appeared Piola, an officer of the Piedmontese Navy, bringing a message from Depretis, whom Garibaldi had left as his Pro-Dictator in Sicily. Depretis urged the Dictator to permit annexation of Sicily to the kingdom of Victor Emmanuel. Generals Türr and Cosenz were present, and helped Piola in his persuasion. Garibaldi agreed to the annexation, and started to dictate a letter to his secretary to that effect. The letter was never finished; for Dr Bertani burst in and persuaded Garibaldi to the contrary. To allow the annexation would be akin to abdicating. Bertani explained that there was no need to fall in with the king's and Cavour's wishes since men and money would be supplied by Sicily and Naples as fast as the provinces were liberated. Türr and Cosenz in vain begged Garibaldi not to listen to the poisonous doctor. One can almost hear Cavour saying to himself: "I told you so."

On 5th September Garibaldi reached Eboli, and Francis II was getting ready to leave Naples. "What an opportunity," lamented Admiral Mundy, "lost for the youngest sovereign in Europe to have made himself a name never to be forgotten in history!" The bravery of his troops at Milazzo should have shown him that they would not desert him if he put himself at the head of them. With that one act of resolution he could have checked the tide of invasion and gained the approbation of the world. The admiral was right. Cavour had not succeeded in bringing about rebellion; most of the troops were loyal in spite of many generals' lack of intrepidity, to put it mildly; and till the end, whether in Capua or Gaeta, the soldiers stuck to and fought for the royal standard. But contrary to the men of the Risorgimento, insipid Francis II was not born at the right moment; and one even wonders whether, if he could have chosen in the annals of history, he could have hit on his right moment.

He issued a proclamation to the Neapolitans in which, among other things, he rightly remarked that his states had been invaded in contravention of the law of nations, notwithstanding that he was at peace with all the European Powers. He less rightly remarked that his throne had been made all the more splendid by the free institutions with which he irrevocably surrounded it. He was referring to the constitution, which, following in his father's footsteps, he had been forced to promulgate. On 6th September he drove down to the Mole; the crowd was indifferent, and the king with his queen, and the ministers of Austria, Prussia, Spain and Bavaria, embarked on the Spanish steamer of war, the *Colón*, and sailed for Gaeta. At the same hour a deputation from the municipality and National Guard of Naples left for Salerno to invite Garibaldi, who needed no invitation, to enter Naples. Francis II's first minister, Liborio Romano, wrote to Garibaldi: "Naples expects with anxiety the invincible Dictator of the Two Sicilies, and confides to him her future destinies."

On 7th September Garibaldi entered Naples. Francis II's Liborio Romano waited for him at the station; for Garibaldi came by rail from Salerno, with General Cosenz and a dozen of his followers. He took up his residence at the Palace of the Foresteria, and addressed the crowd from the balcony at once, and because even in that hour the shrewdness of the Nizzard fisherman did not fail him, he told the Neapolitans to rally round the standard of Victor Emmanuel, the model of all sovereigns, and the true Father of the Italians. He told them in the same breath that Italians from now on would be masters in their own house.

Admiral Persano then paid a visit to Admiral Mundy to tell him that Garibaldi had notified him that after a short rest in Naples he would march against Rome, garrisoned by the French, then on to Venice, which was garrisoned by the Austrians. Persano begged Mundy to use his influence on Garibaldi in dissuading him from his foolhardy undertaking, which could bring immense misfortune on Italy. France and Austria allied would have quickly stamped out all hope for Italia Unita. Admiral Mundy said that though he had nothing to do with political matters he was sure H.M.'s Government would greatly disapprove of any movement against the Austrian possessions. If the opportunity arose he would give his own views to Garibaldi, but all he could do for the moment was to report the conversation to the British minister.

Admiral Mundy went ashore in mufti on 8th September. The people were in ecstasy; men, boys and girls wore every imaginable garment, were armed with swords, spears and flambeaux, and the lazzaroni forced everybody to shout with them, "Evviva Garibaldi!" But there was no drunkenness, order was maintained, and when Garibaldi went to bed word passed among the throng that he was asleep, therefore no noise should disturb him. The Neapolitans became quiet and no sound was heard. No such selfless love, if the story is true, have the Neapolitans shown anyone either before or since.

Mr Elliot, the British minister, received a telegram from Lord John Russell desiring him to express to Garibaldi the hope that no attack would be made on Venice, but as Mr Elliot could not have official communication with the Dictator for the obvious reason that he was still accredited to the Court of Naples, Admiral Mundy called on Garibaldi, who had moved to the Palazzo d'Angri. Garibaldi was lying on a bed in uniform, but wearing easy slippers, which, one trusts, were the slippers Mme Schwartz embroidered for him. He was surrounded by English gentlemen. When Lieutenant Wilmot announced the admiral, Garibaldi remarked that it would not be becoming to receive him without his boots on, and the admiral found him with one boot hastily pulled on as he entered the room.

"I am indeed glad to see you," said Garibaldi. "I told you, Admiral, when we parted at Palermo, that we should meet again at Naples."

There being no chairs in the room they sat down on the

bed. The admiral asked him to come on board the *Hanni-bal* to meet Mr Elliot, who had a message from Lord John Russell for him. Garibaldi said he would be delighted to come, for he considered My Lord Russell "un excellent homme, un véritable ami d'Italie". The admiral was rather surprised at Garibaldi's inside information when the Dictator added that he knew that Monsieur Elliot was connected by marriage with My Lord Russell.

On 10th September Garibaldi and Mr Elliot met on board the *Hannibal*. The Dictator had quite a staff with him, which, naturally, included his evil genius Dr Bertani. Admiral Mundy requested the staff to leave the cabin as the conversation would be private. Bertani objected to Garibaldi being left alone with the British minister and admiral, and stayed behind when the other officers had gone out to the quarter-deck. The admiral insisted on his retiring; he went off reluctantly to join his companions, to watch gunnery exercise.

After complimenting him on the marvellous results he had accomplished Mr Elliot gave him Lord John's message. Garibaldi acquainted them with his plans, for, he thought, he had nothing to hide. He intended to take Rome, then push on to Venice, and added, among other things, that Lord John, in counselling the abandonment of Venice, was not representing the true feelings of England towards Italy. Mr Elliot promptly told him that he misunderstood the feelings of the English nation. The English did not want matters to be pushed so far as to be calculated to bring a European war. Then he spoke of Rome, pointing out the dangers of fighting the French garrison. France would intervene. It was a waste of words since nobody could make Garibaldi see sense if Rome was mentioned. Rome was an Italian city, and neither the Emperor nor anybody else (the Pope) had a right to keep him out of it.

"He was," commented the admiral after the Dictator left, "not to be swayed by any dictates of prudence."

On 11th September, in the afternoon, Admiral Mundy watched the Royal troops evacuating the forts. He saw them march towards Capua, which like Gaeta was still in Neapolitan hands, and though every opportunity was given for desertion from their ranks into the army of the Revolution—as the admiral styled the Garibaldians—only very few availed themselves of it. There was defiance in the men's looks and bearing, which gave no evidence of sympathy with the cause of the Dictator. If Francis II had had a little guts. . . . He had not.

The Neapolitans left behind the gold of the Royal Treasury, and under Bertani's guidance the Garibaldians helped themselves to it by the handful. Gold flowed, the administration of Naples became a very expensive affair, and Dumas, as said before, was not unhelpful in spending it. News reached Garibaldi from Sicily, which was on the verge of anarchy, and only annexation by Victor Emmanuel could have quietened the island. Garibaldi went to Sicily. Depretis was all for annexation, Crispi the Mazzinian against it, and with Bertani at his elbow Garibaldi decided against annexation.

On 17th September another piece of news reached Naples. The Piedmontese troops under General Cialdini had invaded the Papal States. "This invasion," remarked Admiral Mundy, "is a very questionable proceeding." It was.

V

With his great acumen and subtlety Cavour had foreseen what would happen if Garibaldi was let loose and succeeded. The troubles in Sicily, the far from praiseworthy administration of Naples and the South, the refusal of annexation and Garibaldi's plans to attack Rome (which he could not have achieved since it would be seen that he could take neither Gaeta nor Capua) would all help him with Napoleon III. On 28th August Farini and General Cialdini saw the Emperor in Chambéry, and when the plan of invading the Papal States, though leaving Rome strictly alone, and by stopping Garibaldi putting an end to the revolution in the Two Sicilies was laid before him, the Emperor replied: "Bonne chance, et faites vite!" In short Cavour had pulled it off, as he would not only achieve unification, gathering in Umbria and the Marches, but would bring the revolution under control. For Cavour it was important to act quickly. Cialdini acted quick enough for him by violating the Papal frontiers. As some excuse was needed, he issued a proclamation which began: "Soldiers! I am leading you against a band of drunken foreigners whom thirst for gold and a desire for plunder have brought into our country."

The drunken foreigners were the Papal troops under the command of General Christophe Leon Louis Juchault de la Moricière, usually referred to by English and Italian writers as Lamoricière, who was one of France's most respected and best generals, who had been minister of war in France under the régime of General Cavaignac, and a hero of Algeria, and who was an opponent of the policy of Napoleon III. His troops had among them the Franco-Belgian Zouaves and Guides, a *corps d'élite*, almost all of them noblemen, serving without pay, providing their own horses and uniforms, and expected to be in a position of spending from four to five thousand francs of their own a year, and to die for the Holy Father, which many of them would. The Austrians, Swiss and Bavarians were disciplined troops too, and of almost equal enthusiasm. The Italians of the Papal Army had very little enthusiasm:

after all, they would fight, if they fought, against other Italians, whose banner stood for the unification of their country, so they fought as little as possible; but surely they could not have been called foreigners, if not drunks, just to excuse Cialdini for that "very questionable proceeding"?

Since we have spoken of Garibaldi's British Legion, it is worth speaking of some other volunteers, namely St Patrick's Battalion, the Irish volunteers who went to fight and fought for the Pope.

M. T. Crean, who had served as a lieutenant in the Battalion of St Patrick and was severely wounded at Spoleto, said in 1908:

> The British Government, under which Ireland was, and is, whether Liberal or Conservative, sympathized with the Italian movement. The English press and people supported it in the cause of freedom—as with characteristic Pharisaism they called it—but in reality because they recognized in it the downfall of the Catholic Church in Italy. In Ireland the danger to the Head of the Catholic world called forth an enthusiastic spirit, and a desire to help with men and money in the preservation of the independence of the Holy See. They did both. Large sums were subscribed, and a body of 1400 volunteers found their way to Italy.
>
> It was felt by the friends of the Holy Father [goes on M. T. Crean] that, for the preservation of his territory from the Garibaldians, his army should be strengthened. The Papal force was small, and not perhaps as effective as might be desired. The French were occupying Rome and there at all events the Revolutionists dare not stir, but Umbria and the Marches were without an adequate force.

It is worth noting that the Holy See needed volunteers in fear of an invasion by Garibaldi. That the invasion would or could come by the troops of Victor Emmanuel had not entered Papal calculations. It would not have occurred to

Pio Nono that Victor Emmanuel would violate his territory. Hence the Pope's forces were inadequate. Hence, too,
Cialdini had to hurry.

Among the Irish volunteers was a Dublin man called
Abraham John who kept a diary, which he started on
Monday, 14th May 1860. On the 15th he and some
companions were already at Liverpool in the Crooked
Billet Hotel. On the 16th they started on board the *Jester*
from Hull to Antwerp: "Some of us a little sick but
nothing to signify." From Antwerp they went to Malines,
then to Aix-la-Chapelle where they saw the tomb of
Charlemagne, then Cologne, Hanover, Magdeburg, Dres-
den, and they reached Badenbach in Austria on the 21st.

> Washed and breakfasted at 4 o'clock a.m. [says the diary].
> Dined at 1 o'clock. Here Lieut. d'Arcy was to give us up to
> some Austrian officers who were to bring us to Vienna, but
> we would not stand being mixed up with a lot of ignorant
> Kerrymen that were with us from Malines and had almost
> totally disgraced us by their fighting. So ignorant were some
> of them that when at dinner what they wanted to know was
> what they were given the towels (napkins) for and another
> insisted that it was impossible for him to eat raw cabbage
> (salad) they gave him, so there was a regular mutiny and at
> last to pacify us Lieut. d'Arcy had to come with us to Vienna.

While in Vienna Abraham John went to see the Palace
of Schoenbrunn. "This palace surpassed anything that I
have hitherto seen of the kind." On the 25th, fifty-nine
more Kerrymen arrived. On the 28th they left for Trieste,
and sailed next day from Trieste to Ancona "amid the
deafening hurrahs of the Irish and the weak vivas of 300
Belgians that were bound to join the Papal Army. Some of
the Belgians gave some drink to our men and it was with
the greatest difficulty that we could keep the peace."
From Ancona they marched to Loretto, where they heard

Mass at the Cathedral of Our Lady of Loretto. On 6th June part of their kit was issued to the Irish.

There was some trouble on the 9th :

> We were all called at about 2 o'clock this morning on account of one of our officers having told some of the men on guard that Garibaldi had landed with 500 men on the coast about 5 miles from here, so we were all up in a very short time, but as we had no arms the men were alarmed about his coming and catching us in that way. Marched up to Capt. Russell's quarters to know the truth of it to which he sent us word that he knew nothing of it, therefore all returned to the barracks sincerely hoping that when he does come that he will not catch us in the way we were this morning. The tunic we wear at present is a blue one with yellow facings, but the Pope has promised us green ones in a few days.

From Loretto they marched to Rome in the sweltering heat. The peasants did not show the Irish any friendliness, and the Irish in order to show that the peasants were dealing with friends would stop at the entrance of a village and let out a boisterous encouraging cheer; and windows and doors would close and the peasantry would take to the fields.

> In Rome the arrangements for the reception of the Irish volunteers [says Lieut. Crean] were far from perfect, and my recollection of that time is that officials in the service of the government deliberately created difficulties and caused embarrassment. I remember one remarkable instance of this. The men had to undergo a medical examination for the purpose of ascertaining their fitness for military service. The medical gentleman commissioned by the Government to carry this out was an Italian. A number of Tipperary men averaging about six feet in height—perfect types of strength and activity—were rejected by this Italian Doctor. . . . This Doctor was subsequently stated to be deeply implicated in the plots of the Garibaldians.

Eventually both Lieutenant Crean and Abraham John found themselves in Spoleto. The Irish force formed two divisions, one at Ancona and one at Spoleto.

In the early part of September [says Crean] Francis II fled from Naples and Garibaldi entered and assumed the dictatorship of the Kingdom. He even declared his intention of going to Rome, regardless of the fact that the French were in occupation there. This made the situation very embarrassing for Victor Emmanuel, and there was danger that the Great Powers would intervene, but Cavour was equal to the occasion. He sent a request to the Pope to dismiss his army, and before the answer to this message was received, the Piedmontese army—numbering 70,000 men—crossed the pontifical frontier.

Lamoricière had about six thousand men. There was practically no fighting to speak of in Perugia, where some of the Irish were. In Spoleto there was. On 29th September Mr Crean wrote from Genoa to his brother Dr I. J. Crean:

I am a prisoner in Genoa after having gone through a good deal of fighting and fatigue, and quite safe and comfortable, with the exception of the wound in my left arm. I suppose you have seen that Spoleto capitulated, but I dare say the accounts up to this published, have not done anything like justice to the Irish. There were only two companies of Irish and fifteen soldiers of the Franco Belge who did anything. The others Gendarmes and Swiss remained perfectly quiet. At one o'clock we were roused out of bed by the alarm, and all the men were immediately placed on the walls. The attack however did not begin until 7.30 the same morning.

They opened with a tremendous fire. At first the men jumped about and got into disorder, but as they grew accustomed to it they remained quite steady and seemed to think it quite fun. I felt a bit nervous in the outset, but after one or two rounds of shot and shell I did not mind. There were five thousand attacking us, all splendid soldiers who had been in two or three campaigns, and to meet those we had a handful of recruits, half disciplined, and almost worn out from the harassing duty they had to go through for a week before. At three o'clock they charged us with two picked companies of Bersaglieri—supported by two Battalions of Grenadiers, and commanded by the General. The attack was made upon the gate where I was posted with my section. I thought all was over with us. However after a struggle at the gate for a few moments, a discharge of grape from us which had a terrible effect, and heavy fire of musketry from the walls the Piedmontese were driven back with great loss. Out of the Company that came up first to the gate only a few escaped and the second Company of Bersaglieri lost thirty-five between killed and wounded.—They are beyond a question brave men and splendid soldiers. The blows of the axes on the gate were terrific, but fortunately our men shot them down as they came up. It was during this charge that I received the rifle bullet through the arm. I was the only officer wounded though of course the others were in quite as much danger, if not more. At seven o'clock the firing ceased. During the whole day we lost only three killed and nine wounded. The loss on the other side was more than three hundred killed and a large number wounded. This is no exaggeration. I heard it myself from the lips of a Piedmontese officer. The officers are a fine generous set of fellows and treated us along the way here with the greatest possible courtesy. I believe one Company of Irish has been completely cut away at Loreto. . . . It is a curious fact that almost all the men who have been wounded are Tipperary men.

Mr Crean[1] returned to Ireland, was subsequently called to the Irish Bar and was for many years a legal com-

[1] This writer is indebted to Mr Crean's grandson the Very Reverend Cyril P. Crean, Head Chaplain to the Irish Forces, for permission to use the above extracts, and for letting him look at Abraham John's diary.

missioner, Irish Land Commission. He was made a
Cameriere of the Distinguished Order of Pius IX.

Abraham John was taken prisoner too at Spoleto, and
was taken to Genoa, where with his mates he was brought
to a very large barrack, and very well treated considering
they were prisoners. From Genoa they were shipped to
Marseilles, where they "marched to the Barracks allotted
for us without guard as we were no longer prisoners.
Having some money left went to a boarding house to
sleep, of course taking my meals at the barracks which
were good and substantial. Through the city in the evening." On the 25th, already in Paris on their way home, he

> went to see the Place de Concorde and Madeline Chapel. . . .
> Returned to Richfeu's café where we found the place literally
> besieged by people of every class, cutting the buttons off the
> men's coats as mementoes. Was left only two myself. The
> excitement of the French about us and their kind treatment
> will never be forgotten by one of us. I have known a man
> who had not got an opportunity of getting a shave or a change
> of linen since we were taken prisoners, and one woman laid
> hold of him, actually dragging him forcibly into her house
> where she shaved him herself and put clean linen into his
> hands . . . a workman seeing a soiled shirt on a man actually
> took his own off and gave it to him.

Evidently the Parisians did not take them to be drunken
foreigners whom thirst for gold and a desire for plunder
had sent to Italy. Abraham John's last two entries in his
diary are:

> 10th August, 1868 Married Mary Webb.
> „   1869 Mary Jane born.

But the great battle between the Piedmontese and the
Papal troops under Lamoricière was fought at Castelfidardo. On the eve of the battle Count Becdelièvre, the

colonel of the Franco-Belgian tirailleurs, thus addressed
his men: "Tomorrow, at this hour, several among us will
have appeared before God. Now, you know that a man
should be clean when he appears before Him. Let those
who are not so go round to the office of our chaplain. I
have only just left him myself." Lamoricière was proceeding by forced marches to Ancona, but was caught by
the Piedmontese before he could cross the Terni. That
was on the same day, the 17th.

The battle against Cialdini's seventeen thousand men
was fought on the next day. The Franco-Belgians, some
of the Swiss, the Irish and the Austrians fought valiantly,
and they might have got through to Ancona if their
Italian comrades had been a little keener on fighting.
General Pimodan, the second-in-command, was killed in
the battle, and so were many of the Franco-Belgians.
When M. d'Ideville went to the club in Turin a Piedmontese general handed him the list of the French dead
and wounded with the remark: ". . . on croirait lire
une liste d'un petit lever de Louis XIV."

With the remnant of his small force Lamoricière reached
Ancona, which was then invested by land and sea, the
fortress and town falling to the Piedmontese on 28th
September. With that, Papal resistance came to an end,
and the Piedmontese hurried on towards Naples.

Mazzini had turned up in Naples. The population was
not pleased to see him. The good people of Naples wanted
annexation as badly as the Sicilians, and went to shout
under Mazzini's window: "Death to Mazzini!" He
suggested to Garibaldi that he should offer the following
terms to Victor Emmanuel: annexation of Naples in
return for the dismissal of Cavour, and immediate war
with Austria. Bertani, and Crispi, who followed him as
secretary to the Dictator, behaved despotically, the

ministers Garibaldi had appointed on his arrival were bullied and not listened to, and Garibaldi and Bertani issued decrees changing principles of law, finance and civil service. Garibaldi gave a pension to the mother of Agesilao Milano, who had tried to assassinate King Bomba, and by appointing Dumas, his friend and biographer, Director of the National Museum Garibaldi did not endear himself either with the Neapolitans. His administration was high-handed, and worse than that, a failure. Mazzini, Bertani and Crispi were in their element. Garibaldi's hatred of Cavour was constantly fanned by them.

Then came the battle of the Volturno. Garibaldi's admirers say he won it. Be that as it may, both Capua and Gaeta remained in Royalist hands. If the Royalists had had the impetus and the verve and the right strategy they could have chased him to and out of Naples. Garibaldi lost 306 killed, with 1,328 wounded and 389 missing. He took over 2,000 prisoners. During the battle he had to be on the defensive, which never was his *métier*. He had 20,000 men under him; far too many for a guerrillero; but his courage was still that of a guerrillero. Once again everything had gone as Cavour willed it. When silence fell on the battlefield the clock struck with a grinding tired sound; and it dimmed for good Garibaldi's star.

On 8th October, records Admiral Mundy, Bertani, "having failed to give satisfaction to any party, had at last taken his leave, and had proceeded to Turin, where, as a member of the Legislature, he would have opportunity of detailing his grievances before Parliament". Mazzini was still around, much disliked by the Garibaldian generals, most of whom wanted the annexation.

On 14th October the admiral noted with satisfaction that the king had taken command of the army at Ancona on the 9th, had already crossed the frontier into the

Neapolitan dominion, and issued an address to the peoples of Southern Italy. "I have proclaimed Italy for the Italians, and I will not permit Italy to become a focus for Cosmopolitan sects, who may meet there to contrive schemes of reaction or of universal demagogic intrigues. . . . My troops advanced among you to maintain order. . . . As for Italy, I know that there I bring to a close the era of revolutions." That was Cavour's voice, but only the king could enforce it.

Garibaldi issued a proclamation too: "No more political colours, no more discords, no more parties. Italy one, as the people of this metropolis determined it, the king *galantuomo*, are the eternal symbols of our regeneration, and of the grandeur and prosperity of the country." What else could he say with discontent around him, the vast Piedmontese army marching towards him, and no room for private manoeuvres with the fortresses of Capua and Gaeta still in Bourbon hands?

Garibaldi, with some of his staff and men, rode out to meet the king. They met on 26th October. He watched Piedmontese regiments march past, then greeted Generals della Rocca and Cialdini, then there were shouts: "The king is coming!" Garibaldi and his staff rode to the edge of the road, and along the road came Victor Emmanuel on horseback. Garibaldi doffed his hat, shouted loudly: "I salute the first King of Italy." The king held out his hand, they shook hands. The king asked how *caro* Garibaldi was, Garibaldi said he was well, then inquired after the king's health, and the king assured him he was very well.

Admiral Mundy's comment was that "there was sadness in the whole interview. The devotion manifested by the Dictator was altogether personal in character and could in no way solve the increasing difficulties of their public relationship." And truly enough at his first audience of the king Garibaldi urged him to dismiss Cavour. There followed plenty of trouble and bickering, though never with the king, about the fate and pay of the Garibaldians. "It was said in Naples," remarked an Englishman in Naples, "if Garibaldi's troops invaded the Two Sicilies for the sake of pay and promotion, they were no heroes, whatever else they may have been. If they were inspired patriots then the less was said about the inadequacy of the reward to patriotism, the better for the credit of the patriots."

The king went to the Opera House attended by Farini, Admiral Persano, General della Rocca and his personal staff. It had been arranged that Garibaldi should accompany the king, and the audience knew that. But a few minutes before Victor Emmanuel's arrival, the chair that had been placed for Garibaldi on the left of the royal chair was removed by a lackey. That meant Garibaldi would not be coming, and there were plenty of murmurs of disapproval. At that inopportune moment the king entered the royal box. He was in uniform, wearing the star of the grand cross of the Annunciata. He looked and behaved with dignity and severity, and at the end of the opera there was an outburst of popular applause. Nevertheless, he left before the beginning of a new ballet, which had been expressly composed for his edification.

On 8th November he received Garibaldi in audience. Garibaldi said: "Sire, The Neapolitan people in public meeting assembled have proclaimed you their king by an immense majority. Nine million Italians are united to the other provinces ruled over by your Majesty with so much wisdom, and verify your solemn promise that Italy shall belong to the Italians."

Victor Emmanuel made answer in his usual laconic style. With that ended the dictatorship. Mazzini had already bolted. Capua was reduced by the Piedmontese under General della Rocca, and Gaeta held out till February 1861. Francis II and his brave queen took refuge in Rome.

Garibaldi informed his "companions in arms" that: "We shall soon meet again, to march towards the redemption of our brethren, still slaves of the stranger. We shall soon meet again to march together to new victories." On 9th November, at six in the morning, Garibaldi came on board the *Hannibal* to take leave of Admiral Mundy. The admiral was still in his cot, got up, dressed quickly and hurried to his cabin where Garibaldi was waiting for him in red shirt and grey trousers, but without a sword. Through the stern verandah window he pointed to an English merchant vessel, and said sadly:

"There is the ship which is to carry me to my island home; but, Admiral, I could not depart without paying you a farewell visit. It is the last which I make before leaving Naples. Your conduct to me since our first meeting at Palermo has been so kind, so generous, that it can never be erased from my memory. It is engraven there indelibly."

Then he invited the admiral to pay him a visit at his cottage at Caprera, and spoke of the harbour between the island and the main where Nelson had once anchored for the protection of his fleet. Mundy observed that as his time of service would not be up for another eighteen months, he thought it unlikely that in a year and a half he would still find Garibaldi on that tiny island. Garibaldi's mood changed, and he harangued his host on Rome and Venice. Though he preached moderation again, the admiral understood his sentiments about Rome and Venice, but remained bewildered by his inveterate hatred of Cavour. Victor Emmanuel was not mentioned during the interview. Garibaldi wrote some words in the admiral's visiting-book in French reaffirming his gratitude for life. He became dejected again and, says the admiral, "his whole manner was that of a man who was suffering a poignant grief".

The visit lasted twenty minutes, then Garibaldi was rowed by four boys to the *Washington*, which sailed with him in a few hours' time.

"Giuseppe Garibaldi," cried a patriot, "after having accomplished his heroic work, all he took with him into the solitude of Caprera was a sackful of vegetables and dried codfish. Those were his only spoils of war."

FROM CAPRERA TO CAPRERA

I

"WELL would it have been if the ship *Washington*," wrote an English wellwisher of Garibaldi, "which bore Garibaldi to Caprera had taken him away from Italy never to return. He would then have died a glorious man; there would have been left nothing but a splendid career for the historian to relate."

There were no more splendours in store for him.

Garibaldi stayed in Caprera for a while, and was visited by English noblemen, old companions in arms, and one day to please him two visiting Prussian officers carried stones for him till their backs ached. The king sent by General Türr a diamond necklace for his daughter Teresa, and soon Teresa would marry Stefano Canzio, who was as rabid a revolutionary as she could ask for. The Solitary, as Garibaldi liked to call himself, urged Bertani from the seclusion of Caprera to prepare for further mischief. By the spring Italy must have a million patriots in arms.

Elected as deputy to the Chamber, he went in April 1861 to Turin to make his contribution to Parliament. He spent the first five days in Turin without condescending to go to the Chamber. He gave his often-recurring painful rheumatism as an excuse for staying away; and while he stayed away Turin filled with Garibaldians, and Bertani arrived with his Genoa Committee. It became known that on 18th April Garibaldi would speak in the Chamber. Garibaldians filled the galleries early in the morning. There were large crowds outside too. The diplomatic gallery was also full. Among the diplomats sat the very observant M. d'Ideville. He had a word with Sir James Hudson, the British minister, who had seen Cavour, to whom he was devoted, though once or twice Cavour had double-crossed him too—but only in diplomacy and politics. "Though Cavour seemed very calm this morning," said Sir James, "I am afraid." Sentries were doubled everywhere because of the Garibaldians, who crammed the town. Moreover, many dubious people had come to Turin in their wake. At 1.30 p.m. the President of the Chamber, Rattazzi, took his seat. All the ministers were present. Towards two o'clock vociferous cheers outside heralded Garibaldi's approach. It was taken up by the Garibaldians filling the galleries; there were shouts too.

Garibaldi entered through a small, almost hidden door, wearing red shirt, grey poncho, and M. d'Ideville, who saw him for the first time, thought he looked like a prophet or an old comedian. All the deputies, except about fifteen of the extreme Left, remained seated. There were even louder cheers from the public galleries. M. d'Ideville was struck by the icy coldness of the deputies compared to the howling galleries, which, he noted, contained no Turinese. Garibaldi sat down on the extreme left with two deputies, who had accompanied him. When Baron Ricasoli finished with the interpellations about the volunteers, General Fanti, the war minister, who had no love for Garibaldi, spoke firmly on the subject of the volunteers Garibaldi had left in Naples and Palermo, some of whom had been incorporated into the Royal army, the rest disbanded. When he sat down, Garibaldi rose to speak. There was great emotion in the Chamber since everybody knew of his implacable hatred for Cavour.

Garibaldi, d'Ideville found, completely swollen-headed

by Neapolitan ovations, was arrogant with the government, and because of his treating the king as an equal, you could see that he was very unpopular in monarchist Turin, and considered dangerous. His courage and honesty were admired, but nobody in Turin ignored his stupidity and weak character. M. d'Ideville thought that Garibaldi had something of the lion in his face, but did not like his small eyes. The voice was sonorous, the red shirt and poncho made him look theatrical.

Alas, the actor did not know his part. He was incoherent, fumbled among the papers before him. Even the binoculars he held in his hand were of no help to him. However hard he tried he could not get going, in spite of his two acolytes whispering the sentences to him and pointing at the sheets of paper before him. All effort was useless.

It was going badly. The Garibaldian deputies were deeply embarrassed because of the deplorable impression their chief was making. Suddenly Garibaldi pushed the papers away, and started to improvise and shout. Turning from ridiculous to tragic, the scene changed completely. In a threatening voice, accompanied by similar movements, he shouted at the ministerial bench that he could never take the hand of a man who sold his country to the foreigner, and made an alliance with a government whose cold and evil hand had endeavoured to foment fratricidal war. That was a reference to Napoleon III, for having agreed to the king taking over the ex-dictator's Two Sicilies.

On those words of the ex-dictator the whole House rose to its feet. The Garibaldians cheered loudly in the galleries. Cavour, who had listened so far coldly, turned pale and trembled with anger. A Left-wing deputy hurled himself at the ministerial bench and threatened the president with his fist. The president shouted at him. Some deputies of the Right dragged him away. Noise and tumult grew, and there were shouts even at the diplomatic gallery from deputies of the Left.

Rattazzi, the president, did not behave with outstanding courage. When Garibaldi used the word treason, all he did was to look away. He seemed very embarrassed and during the twenty minutes of pandemonium did nothing to restore order. When the noise subsided he called on Garibaldi to continue with his speech. The deputies shouted, "Order! Order!" Rattazzi asked Garibaldi to moderate his speech. The partisans cheered Garibaldi as he rose. He appeared completely impervious to the storm he had raised. He spoke in the same vein as before.

After him that firebrand Nino Bixio rose, and surprisingly for him asked the Chamber to forgive his chief, who was more a warrior than an orator. Bixio then pleaded for concord among Italians. The Left, says M. d'Ideville, did not care for his speech because of the "*brevet d'imbécillité*" he accorded Garibaldi.

Cavour was labouring under emotion when he rose to speak. He spoke in complete silence, spoke only of concord, asked the deputies to let bygones be bygones, and made no allusion to Garibaldi's outrageous words and his ingratitude. Garibaldi rose to speak again. Everybody expected that, moved by such generosity, he would accept the nobly offered hand. Not Garibaldi. He accused and recriminated just as vulgarly as before, then announced that he could reconcile himself with the government only if he were given command of the Army of the South. (Cheers and counter-cheers.) "Has not England this moment," he bellowed, "a volunteer army? Have we not more enemies than England? Is not Austria on the defensive and are not the French of Rome our enemies?"

When Garibaldi got over his wrath, he said: "I am sure Count Cavour loves his country. Let him, therefore, use his influence in support of my bill for arming the country. Let the volunteers of the Army of the South be recalled into service."

M. d'Ideville left the chamber convinced that Cavour's conciliatory tone averted civil war in Italy. Events were to prove that his surmise was wrong; for Garibaldi had neither the influence nor the desire to bring it about. The king arranged a meeting in Moncalieri between Cavour and Garibaldi. Cavour was the more ready to make peace, and first to offer his hand. Yet he had every reason to be disgusted with him. Apart from anything else, Cavour assisted Garibaldi's family in distress while he was in America. Garibaldi went to Moncalieri to please the king; his attitude to Cavour remained unchanged.

Dumas arrived in Turin in the course of the spring bringing an introduction from Garibaldi to the king. "Sire," wrote Garibaldi simply, "do receive Dumas. He is your friend and mine. G. Garibaldi." That was not, however, treating the king as an equal: it was being Garibaldi.

The spring began to turn into the hot Piedmontese summer and early in June Italy suffered a heavy blow. On 6th June 1861 Victor Emmanuel went to the sick-bed of Cavour, who had suddenly been taken gravely ill. The king remained at the door of the sick-room without moving. The dying Cavour recognized him. "Ah! Maestà!" he said. They were then left alone. Ten minutes later Victor Emmanuel left in tears. When the agony set in, Cavour said repeatedly: "Empereur! Italie! Pas d'état de siège!" He recovered consciousness in the night, turned to his nephew and asked:

"The doctors have given me up, have they not?"

His sister the Marchesa Alfieri said, "No, not at all."

"Well," said Cavour, "it is I who will give them up tomorrow."

Fortified by the last rites of the Church he had despoiled,
Cavour died in the morning. The whole of Italy mourned,
yet not one word came from Caprera.

Garibaldi was busy on his island with visitors who came
to adulate him, among them an Englishwoman, Caroline
Giffard Philipson, who wrote poems to him, the first
entitled "To Giuseppe Garibaldi", the second, "A Christ-
mass Greeting", the third, "To My Friend". He was also
busy with the idea of a universal language, which, he said,
could be of more help than religion. It would have three
ingredients: French, English and German. That would
be only for Europeans and Americans. The Orientals
should turn to somebody who had more knowledge of
Oriental languages than he. The new language should be
taught to the young, who would then consider it their
own language—or something.

An old comrade in arms, Colonel Vecchi, gives us a
vivid picture of Garibaldi in Caprera. He went to stay
with him, and on the first evening he found himself at
dinner beside an English nobleman, who had come
expressly to make Garibaldi's acquaintance, and had made
the voyage direct from London in his yacht. Two ample
dishes with young salted blackbirds with beans cooked in
oil were served, followed by blackbirds, minced and fried
in batter. Dried figs, raisins and cheese completed the
meal.

Afterwards Vecchi met his host's donkeys. One was
called Francesco Giuseppe after the Emperor of Austria,
another Pio Nono. Somebody or other had given Pio
Nono a beating. Fruscianti, Garibaldi's factotum, spoke to
the donkey, saying: "It is quite right to take away your
temporal power, but it is wicked to flay you. In '49 we
tried to make you understand, but you would not. You
chose to be independent with the Austrians on one side,

and the French on the other. See what has undone you?
The indignation of the people." Then the herdsman came
up, and he too spoke to the donkey, saying he had been
bitten by another donkey because they were having a fight
over the Immaculate Conception. In short a good time was
had by all. Vecchi was convinced that if the Pope sought
refuge in Caprera Garibaldi would treat him graciously.

Vecchi admired his leader's philosophy too. Garibaldi
said: "The great Spirit of eternal Life is in everything!
These plants, these fruit trees, even these hard granite
rocks have a soul. It may be rudimentary—but there it is.
Do not geologists speak of affinity among metals? Botan-
ists of love among the plants? . . . Plants are speechless;
stones motionless; but I believe they speak a language,
although we are unable to understand it. . . ." Then
Garibaldi would speak of the Pope and his temporal
power, comparing it to the oidium, the disease that
destroys the vine, and he and Vecchi proposed the same
remedy for both: sulphur. When Vecchi left the island he
took bits of stone because his friends ardently wished to
possess something from Caprera. He asked his adored
chief whether he could take them with him. "Please
yourself," said Garibaldi laughing, "I shall be sure to have
too many left."

To the Ladies Association in Genoa Garibaldi wrote:
"To liberate woman from superstition and to release her
from the clutches of the priest, is now a question of life or
death to Italy." But chatting, writing and entertaining
were not enough. There was Rome, which he must simply
wrench from the Pope, and beyond Rome was Venice,
still under Austrian rule. Both Rome and Venice would
belong to Victor Emmanuel in time, but without Garibaldi
having anything to do with it. He could not know that,
besides would never perceive that history had switched its

course away from him. On 3rd March 1862 Garibaldi appeared in Turin. Rattazzi was the prime minister now. Ricasoli's government had just fallen.

Garibaldi had disliked Baron Ricasoli, so he decided to like Rattazzi, whom he went to see, and though nothing ever transpired of their interview it was supposed in Turin that they talked over a project for attacking Austria on the Danube. Kossuth was to go, apparently, to Hungary, lead an insurrection there while Garibaldi was to effect a landing on the coast of Dalmatia. At any rate Garibaldi left Turin satisfied and embarked on one of his triumphal progresses, calling on the population to collect money and arms, and started to enrol volunteers without even telling them why they were enrolled. They knew that if Garibaldi called them then it would mean either Venice or Rome. He informed his friends, however, that he intended to make a landing in Dalmatia. His friends tried to dissuade him from leaving Italy under any pretext whatever. His enemies in Italy, they argued, would be only too glad if they could so easily get rid of him. One thing was certain, namely that for once the king truly knew nothing about the plan. Garibaldi's friends pointed out to him that not only would it be sheer madness to make the attempt, but the volunteers would be arrested before they reached the Venetian frontier. (Victor Emmanuel's hands were tied since Napoleon was absolutely opposed to any attack on Venice.) And, the friends argued, if he made the attempt the Moderates would use it as a pretext for dissolving the rifle clubs and committees set up by the Garibaldians.

Garibaldi was convinced that the government would shut their eyes and allow him a free hand. On 5th May he summoned his friends to Trescone near Brescia to discuss the matter. The friends included Bertani and Jessie White's husband, Mario. They opposed his plans.

Garibaldi became very angry and accused Mario of being a Mazzinian. Mario replied he was neither a Mazzinian nor a Garibaldian, but thought with his own head. The meeting was adjourned to the following day when Garibaldi gave in, that is to say he gave up his designs on Venice, and promised he would think twice before quitting Italy with his volunteers.

Rattazzi must have been warned that the enlistments going on were not destined for Dalmatia but for Venice, but instead of advising the king to summon Garibaldi and to tell him clearly that no attempt on Venice would be countenanced, he had Francesco Nullo, the patriot-poet, and other volunteers arrested, and when they tried to break out of the prison of Brescia the king's soldiers fired on the crowd, killing and wounding some. Garibaldi immediately remonstrated with the prefect and told him as Nullo and the others were his volunteers he too should be arrested. He was not; then he quarrelled with his generals Bixio, Medici and Cosenz, resigned the presidency of the Emancipation Committee, and went back to sulk in Caprera.

In the Chamber an inquiry was called for. The debate was violent, but there was, however, no inquiry. On 28th June Garibaldi suddenly arrived in Palermo. The sons of the king were at the opera house in Palermo on that night. They sat down in a box, saw that the place was empty, asked what had happened and were told that Garibaldi had arrived in Sicily.

Garibaldi got busy. He was, after all, in the seat of his glory. He had gone from Palermo triumphantly to Naples; so it was logical that he should go from Palermo to Rome this time. He was in a garrulous, attacking mood. At a meeting he declared there were only two men in Italy who would never deceive them: Victor Emmanuel and himself. He went to Marsala. There he said; "Shortly, yes, shortly, Rome is ours. Yes, Rome. Rome or death."

Sicily resounded with the "Inno Garibaldi". Without its strains now Garibaldi could not take a step; and his two sons would spend entire nights amusing themselves by listening ad infinitum to it. Those martial strains became part and parcel of the Italian air. After the Second World War, for instance, the Italian Communist Party adopted it as their signature tune. The stirring cry of "*Va fuora d'Italia va fuora o stranier!*" (Go from Italy, go, O stranger) they applied to De Gasperi, who was born in foreign-ruled Trento in the same way as Garibaldi was born in foreign-ruled Nice.

Garibaldi continued to harangue the Sicilians. Napoleon was the real enemy of Italy: the Pope was the enemy of true religion. He remembered the Hungarians whom he had intended to help. On 26th July he published in Palermo a revolutionary address to them. Among other things he said: "Do not forget that in 1848 you had only to push on your triumphal road to Vienna to destroy for ever the old sanguinary throne of the Habsburgs. . . . Italy loves you as a brother . . . she invokes you in the name of the holy fraternity of peoples, in the name of the welfare of all. . . . Will you fail to join the rendezvous of nations when they meet to do battle against despotism?"

The Hungarian general Klapka, the last of the Hungarian generals of the '48 to surrender to the Austrians, answered him from Turin: "General.—You have just addressed an appeal to arms to Hungary. Your voice might have found an echo among my countrymen if you had raised that war-cry at the head of your Volunteers united to the Royal troops to advance by common agreement against the Habsburg dynasty. It cannot now be responded to, for it is not the voice of Italy, but of a man who is working to destroy his own glory, and who compromises his name and his fortune in the sad chances of civil war. . . . Have you not forgotten it, General, by separating yourself, as you have done, from the legal powers sanctioned by the vote of the people and by raising the standard of rebellion?"

In his address to the Hungarians Garibaldi had suggested that Hungary should follow the example of Montenegro, Serbia and Greece. General Klapka bluntly asked him in his reply why he did not go to their help. "What a fine occasion you have lost of continuing the task of liberator."

But the misguided man, as his apologists began to refer to Garibaldi, heeded nobody. It would be Rome, and all this talk about civil war and rebellion was just words, and once he reached Rome everything would be forgiven and he would be hailed as the liberator of Italy's capital. And frankly he could not be blamed. Two years earlier the Sicilian campaign began in a similar manner. Then, too, the authorities pretended they did not approve. Blame by rights should be attached for what followed to Victor Emmanuel and the late Count Cavour; and who could blame a simple-minded man of fervour like Garibaldi for not having perceived that for, to him, nebulous reasons 1862 could not be the same as 1860? Moreover, when he crossed over to the mainland the king's two men-of-war the *Duca di Genoa* and the *Maria Adelaide* left the Straits and proceeded to sea. Did that not look like encouragement, or like looking away at least?

He and his followers crossed over in two steamers, the *General Abbalucci* and the *Dispaccio*. During the crossing the *Maria Adelaide* spoke to them, then sheered off. They landed on the mainland and the advance towards Rome, so he believed, began.

The king sent General Cialdini to stop and arrest Garibaldi. Cialdini looked forward to it. Officers of the regular army, monarchists and moderates by then truly loathed the man who considered himself a law unto himself. The Garibaldians said Cialdini was a mean, cruel traitor. His troops met the Garibaldians at Aspromonte on 29th August.

"Viva Italia! Viva Garibaldi!" shouted the Garibaldians. "Viva Italia! Viva il Re!" shouted the Royal troops.

I divided my troops into two columns [reported Colonel Pallavicino to General Cialdini], that on the right commanded by Lieut.-Col. Parrochia, the left by the Colonel of the 4th Regiment, Chevalier Eberhard. The two columns appeared at the same time in view of the Garibaldian encampment, already abandoned by him, he having taken up a position on the crest of a rugged hillock, to the east of the plateau of Aspromonte. I then sent an order to the commandant of the left column to attack the Garibaldians in front, while making the right column fall back, by a rapid movement I attacked the left flank of the near rebels, in order to cut off their retreat. In the meantime with a battalion I caused the entrance of the valley to be occupied, that they might not regain the plateau. The left column, with the 6th Battalion of Bersaglieri at their head, then attacked the rebels, and after a smart fire carried the position at the point of the bayonet with cries of "Viva il Re! Viva Italia!", while the left side was also attacked by our troops. General Garibaldi and his son Menotti having been wounded and the rebels being surrounded on all sides, resistance became useless, so General Garibaldi gave the signal to cease firing.

Yes, Garibaldi was wounded. "The great crime, the great sacrilege," moaned Jessie White, "had been committed." Colonel Pallavicino knelt beside her wounded hero beseeching him to surrender. Garibaldi gave him his sword, and he was carried away on a stretcher to a peasant's cottage. Cialdini, she tells us, from the bridge of the *Stella d'Italia*, "stood with covered head and folded arms, exultingly watching the departure of his hatred rival, defeated, wounded and a prisoner."

Garibaldi was put on the *Duca di Genoa* and shipped to Spezia. He was far from subdued. "They thirsted for blood," he wrote in a letter that was made public, "and I wished to spare it. Not the poor soldiers who obeyed but the men of the clique who cannot forgive the Revolution for being the Revolution—it is that which disturbs their conservative digestion. . . . Yes, they thirsted for blood. I perceived it with sorrow and I endeavoured in consequence to the utmost to prevent that of our assailants to be shed. . . . I once again present to Italy a serene front, assured of having done my duty." As a matter of fact it was Menotti's column that opened fire first.

Garibaldi suffered agony with his wound on board the *Duca di Genoa*. There was neither ice nor remedies, and the wounded foot became so swollen and inflamed that it was impossible to ascertain whether the bullet was still in the wound or not. On landing, Garibaldi was removed as prisoner to the fortress of Varignano. It was not harsh imprisonment. Crowds of women came to visit him, English, German, Italian, all to adore him and eager to do anything he wanted, and even more eager to take home some souvenir of him. They wanted locks of his hair, and his nail-parings too were much sought after as mementoes. A young soldier in attendance whose hair was of similar colour was shaven almost bald to supply the need for Garibaldi's hair. One of the doctors, Dr Prandina, had to dress one day in a red shirt and lie down on a bed in a dark room to impersonate the hero. William Ashurst came from London to see Garibaldi, saying they were indignant in London because a royal bullet had struck the great

man. He was allowed, of course, to see Garibaldi, and
an English surgeon was sent for. When Dr Parkins
arrived he looked round the prisoner's sick-room and
remarked: "Too many doctors and too many women."
The bullet was extracted, and the glad tidings was telegraphed all over the world.

"We have seen Garibaldi this morning," wrote Mr
Stansfield, who had come too, to Jessie, "the most ex-
quisite and touching sight I ever saw: thin, feeble, with a
smiling, grateful, most prayerful look as he looked up
from his bed and took my hand in his; half child, half
martyr was what he seemed."

On 5th October Garibaldi and his followers of Aspromonte were amnestied. They had behaved, after all, no
worse than two years ago. "Sire," wrote Rattazzi to the
king, "the causes which have hitherto induced your government to counsel you to resist the generous impulse of
your heart towards General Garibaldi and his accomplices
have ceased to exist. The empire of the law is being everywhere consolidated; confidence in the frank and prudent
policy which you have inaugurated has tempered the
impatience which drove the General into rebellion."

The General went back to Caprera convinced that the
king and his government had let him down at Aspromonte.

II

In March 1864 Garibaldi went to England. He was under
the impression that he was invited by the British government. It was not the case; the government knew that
his reception would be enthusiastic; the government
knew too that England's ally Napoleon would not like it..
"To leave Garibaldi in the hands of the British democracy," said Jessie White, whose father's widow was one
of the first on Garibaldi's visiting list, "to allow what they

could not prevent—a triumphal tour through the provinces—did not exactly suit the views of the English aristocracy, who, wise in their generation, therefore took the matter in their own hands."

Garibaldi arrived at Southampton on board the *Ripon*. Lord Palmerston thought it of great importance to make Garibaldi's visit a strictly private one, and suggested that Garibaldi should for reasons of health decline all public dinners "at which he would say foolish things and other people mischievous ones". Garibaldi went to the Isle of Wight and stayed with Mr Seely at Brooke House. Tennyson invited him to plant a tree in his garden and recited to him some of his poetry. Then Garibaldi recited Foscolo's *I Sepolcri*, of which Tennyson understood not a word. Tennyson's opinion of him was that his manners had a certain divine simplicity in them and were gentler than those of most young maidens he knew.

Holyoake saw him there. When Garibaldi with all Mr Seely's guests, who were illustrious personages, returned to Southampton Holyoake heard from some members of Parliament on board that a hundred thousand men were to file before Garibaldi at Nine Elms. That would have meant standing for five hours while the men went past. Mr W. E. Forster, M.P., when a wish was expressed that a less tiring arrangement should be made, turned to Holyoake and said: "Holyoake, you do it." He sent a telegram to London to personal friends at the head of the procession: "If the 100,000 persons, as reported here, are to file past the General at Nine Elms, he will have to stand five hours. He will be weary; his entry into London will be delayed till dusk. If practicable let the General go first, and the procession follow and defile before him at Stafford House." Garibaldi was to be the Duke of Sutherland's guest in London.

In the train Holyoake noticed a vain Italian tradesman of London, who had done nothing to help the cause of the General yet put himself forward as representing the Italians of the metropolis. That Mr Negretti was an enemy of Mazzini to boot. Therefore he was hostile to Holyoake. He got Mr Seely to agree to Holyoake's removal from the train. Holyoake sat in the press carriage, Garibaldi and Menotti with Mr Seely, who was member of Parliament for Lincoln. The station-master who tried to remove Holyoake was a Mr Godson. When he tried to remove Holyoake, who represented the *Newcastle Daily Chronicle* and the *Morning Star*, not one of his journalist colleagues came to his rescue, even though he had paid the hotel bill of one of them, and had sent at the cost of fifteen shillings a telegram for another. He appealed to Mr Forster.

"Please speak to Mr Godson," begged Holyoake, "and tell him that an English member of the press cannot be removed from a public train at the instigation of a foreigner. A word from you, a member of Parliament, will prevent this."

"I cannot interfere," said Mr Forster, turning away.

The station-master tried to prevent Holyoake from returning to his carriage. Holyoake had a good mind to leap into the General's carriage; he would not have allowed him to be removed. Eventually Mr Godson permitted him to continue in the train on the condition that he left it at Nine Elms and did not go on to London. The station of Nine Elms was in the possession of the police. The enthusiastic crowd was endless. Nothing like it would be seen till the coming of Liberace in the nineteen-fifties.

"In a minute," related Holyoake, speaking of their arrival, "I was nearly under horses' feet in the midst of the mighty throng. Here I found a number of carriages waiting. I was invited by the Garibaldi Committee to take

a seat with them, but I preferred the private carriage of a
friend. . . . Without perceiving it the carriage I had
chosen was next to the General's, and thus, without any
intention of my own, I rode right before Garibaldi in the
centre of the mighty throng, which lined the road all the
way to the Duke of Sutherland."

The Italian Embassy and the Italian Moderates of London
kept aloof from Garibaldi's visit. The ambassador d'Azeglio
nephew of the man who refused to arm the Thousand
against a friendly state, openly expressed his surprise and
disgust that England should thus applaud a rebel to his
king.

No picture of Garibaldi in London could be complete
without quoting Lord Malmesbury, who wrote on 13th
April, two days after Garibaldi's triumphal entry:

> We dined at Stafford House to meet Garibaldi; the party
> consisted of the Russells, Palmerstons, Argylls, Shaftesburys,
> Dufferins, Gladstones, &c., the Derbys and ourselves being
> the only Conservatives, so I greatly fear we have made a mis-
> take and that our party will be disgusted at our going. Lady
> Shaftesbury told me after dinner in a *méchante* manner that
> we had fallen into a trap, to which I answered that I was very
> much obliged to those who had laid it, as I should be very
> sorry not to have seen Garibaldi. The Dowager Duchess of
> Sutherland walked off with him to her boudoir, where he
> smoked. This created great astonishment and amusement, as
> this particular boudoir, which is fitted up most magnificently
> with hangings of velvet and everything that is most costly,
> has been considered such a sacred spot that few favoured
> mortals have ever been admitted to its precincts, and as to
> allowing anyone to smoke in it, it is most astounding to all
> who know the Duchess.

The Dowager Duchess of Sutherland wrote Garibaldi
gushing letters, which were reproduced in Curatulo's

Garibaldi e le Donne. They were written, he tells us, in indifferent French, which he translated into good Italian, thus it would be somewhat ludicrous to try to reproduce them in the language in which she thought them out. Many of Garibaldi's close friends believed for a while that he would marry her. His friends, however, as we know, were at times willing to believe anything.

Holyoake was at a crowded party in Fulham where both Garibaldi and Mazzini were present. Mazzini contended that no atheist could have a sense of duty.

"What do you say to me?" asked Garibaldi at once. "I am an atheist. Do I lack the sense of duty?"

"Ah," said Mazzini playfully, "you imbibed duty with your mother's milk."

Mazzini also remarked at the time that Garibaldi looked like a lion; and did not a lion have a stupid expression?

Garibaldi, leaving the ducal splendours of Stafford House, went to a banquet where almost all the celebrated agitators were present. He called on Louis Blanc and Ledru-Rollin and the British government became rather embarrassed by it all. As a result of that the Duke of Sutherland became "seriously concerned for Garibaldi's health", so he summoned the famous surgeon Fergusson, who diagnosed in respect of Garibaldi's intended triumphal tour round England (like Lombardy in 1859) "the fatigue and excitement of the proposed tour would be fraught with danger". That did not discourage Garibaldi, who never feared danger, so Mr Gladstone spoke to him and, so says Jessie White Mario, "Mr Gladstone revealed to him that in spite of so many official receptions, dinners and addresses, his presence was really an embarrassment to the Government. This interview greatly troubled and grieved the simple-minded General." The upshot was that

Garibaldi, after visiting Colonel Pearce in Cornwall, left England in the Duke of Sutherland's yacht.

"The end of his visit to England," wrote Holyoake, "was sudden, unforeseen, inexplicable both to friend and foe at the time and for long after."

III

The spirit of Cavour kept marching on. When in 1866 war between Austria and Prussia became imminent, Italy decided to take Venice, since Austria now seemed an easy prey. On 18th June the Italian prime minister Baron Ricasoli declared in the Chamber: "The Kingdom of Italy has declared war against the Empire of Austria." The reason was given in the King's Order of the Day to the Army: "Austria by arming on our frontiers incites us to war again. In my name and that of the nation I call you to arms."

It looked easy, mighty easy; nevertheless the Italian army under General La Marmora was smartly beaten by the Austrians commanded by the Archduke Albert at Custozza, where Radetzky had defeated Victor Emmanuel's ill-fated father in 1848. Victor Emmanuel, however, was not ill-fated in spite of a second resounding defeat in the naval battle of Lissa. The action was fought between Admirals Tegethoff and Persano. Persano was put under arrest after the battle. But Austria lost to Prussia, thus Italy won too. Austria, in order to show her disdain, gave Venice to Napoleon, who then made Italy a present of it.

Before the war began Victor Emmanuel and his advisers decided to forget that Garibaldi was a mischievous rebel, who had fought his king at Aspromonte and who had been cold-shouldered ever since. He was asked to form a volunteer corps, take command of it, and was sent back to his wonted battleground, that is the lakes nearest to Austria. It was not anything like '48 and '59 this time. None the less, Garibaldi claimed many small victories, adding to his long list of the past, Lodrone, Darso, Condino, Ampola and Bezzecca. He went on to attack Trento, but was recalled by General La Marmora. "*Obedisco*," telegraphed Garibaldi for a change. On the brief war he commented in his novel *Rule of the Monk*: "She, Venice, emerges from foreign dominion, not through her own acts, but by the courage of others. Oh! if only her liberty had been won by the valour of her brethren! But no, she was redeemed by foreign swords. Sadowa, the glory of Prussia, freed Venice, and the Italian nation asks no veil to hide this dishonour." He went back to Caprera.

In the spring of 1867 he went to Florence, where he was joined by the inextinguishable Mme Schwartz, who had just arrived from Crete. She found his charm as indefinable as it was irresistible, but he seemed tired and unnerved. He complained to her that he could stay no longer on the mainland because he was importuned without mercy. He confessed to her that his health was much impaired. He made her feel his arm. "See," he said, "how thin I am. I am better now; but a short time ago I was obliged to keep my bed for three days on account of my rheumatism, and my Aspromonte wound remained open for six months." It pained her to hear him talk that way, and when he wanted to rest she rose immediately from the sofa.

She went to Switzerland in September to the Peace Congress of the International Society of Peace and Liberty, which he was to open. Garibaldi had to go by train because the steamboat company, which was under French influence, refused passage to the committee. She met him at the Hotel Biron, in Villeneuve, where she

found him at table with a number of friends. He was in
good spirits, but did not walk any the more easily, and
looked as tired as ever. His thinned and white locks
harmonized only too well with the pallor of his features.
He was still wearing grey trousers, red shirt and poncho.
She asked him after his family.

"Menotti is in Florence," said the delegate to the Peace
Congress. "As for Ricciotti, I have sent him to England
to collect money among my friends for the overthrow of
the Papacy." But he did, so he told her, do what he could
to prevent the execution of the Emperor Maximilian.

The train was about to start. The crowd shouted, "Vive
Garibaldi!" It was drowned, Mme Schwartz regretted,
more than once by cries of "Vive la République Uni-
verselle!" and "Vive la République Européenne!" Garibaldi capped that by shouting: "Vive Genève, la Rome de
l'intelligence!" A saloon carriage was put at his disposal.
Mme Schwartz was dissatisfied with the journey from
Villeneuve to Geneva; for "with the exception of the
little town of Morges, where flags fluttered over the high-
way, where cannons were fired, hymns sung, and speeches
delivered, and where Garibaldi had to wet his lips with the
wine of the cup of honour; and, with the exception of
Saint-Prex and Allaman, where also some little enthusiasm was shown, the presence of Garibaldi left his enter-
tainers somewhat unmoved." She consoled herself with
the thought that in his room would be waiting the finest
peaches, pears and grapes of the market, which she had
bought for him, next to her yearly gift of a cap embroidered by her own hands. He was infuriated by a Swiss
ecclesiastic who had dared to tell him that in the presence
of God he, Garibaldi, was but a weak servant.

"Since these gentlemen will preach to me," he said to
Mme Schwartz, "I must tell you plainly what I also

think: I see that the Protestant clergy are as bigoted as the Catholics—they are all the same, as far as I am concerned." "*È tutt' una bottega*", was what he said in Italian. In Geneva itself he received a triumphal reception. Now satisfied, Mme Schwartz left Switzerland and the Peace Congress to Garibaldi.

From the Peace Congress he moved almost at once against Rome, that is to say he rebelled again, believing that it would get him to Rome, which he would then give to Victor Emmanuel and Italy. He went from Florence, accompanied by a magazine of arms, to Asinalunga by way of Arezzo, but there he was arrested by the government. Garibaldi considered, and said, it was ridiculous to arrest him for having spent a night among friends some fifteen miles from the Roman frontier. He was taken to the citadel of Alessandria, then was set free, and when he expressed the desire to return to Caprera a warship was placed at his disposal. He was given military honours when he left Alessandria on 28th September, and was not stopped when he made a speech to the soldiers about Rome, the capital of Italy.

After a week in Caprera the Solitary had enough of solitude and took ship for Leghorn. There he was arrested and shipped back to Caprera. A warship was sent there for the sole purpose of keeping watch on him. On 14th October the tenacious old guerrillero escaped from the island in a boat, and on the 20th his volunteers were with him again. He issued a proclamation against France and the Pope, and crossed the Roman frontier at Passo Corese. He had about seven thousand men, and the first engagement took place at Monterotondo. The Garibaldians entered the town. (The French were to refer to it as Montre-ton-dos, for only the backs of the Garibaldians were to be seen after their defeat at Mentana.) General

Kanzler, in command of the Papal troops, counter-attacked, but his men were driven back.

Garibaldi was hoping to take Rome by a *coup de main* before French reinforcements could arrive. Victor Emmanuel was furious. "Europe knows," he declared, "that the standard raised in our neighbour's territory, on which is written the destruction of the supreme spiritual authority of the head of the Catholic Church, is none of ours." Cialdini was sent after Garibaldi again. "War with our ally would be fratricide," said the king too, thinking of French reaction.

The French marched up from Civitavecchia and Garibaldi had to retreat from the position he took up by the Mentana bridge. Garibaldi in retreat! Five thousand volunteers immediately deserted. On 3rd November his vanguard was suddenly attacked by the Papal Zouaves. That took Garibaldi by surprise, but he rallied his troops. The small Papal force held out till the French arrived, and Garibaldi was defeated. When his troops took to their heels he shouted at them: "Sit down and you will win." At four in the afternoon he observed: "This is a battle between people who run away and people who don't advance." Then with his officers and his two sons he crossed the frontier back into Italy, leaving behind wounded, dead, a thousand prisoners and pillaged churches. He maintained that he had lost because the Romans betrayed him by neither rising nor giving him intelligence of the position and advance of the French. At Passo Corese he got into a special train to Florence. Now that the little matter was over he felt like going back to a well-deserved rest in Caprera. At the station of Frigline the train was stopped by a battalion of Bersaglieri.

Lieut.-Col. Camozzi of the carabinieri went into Garibaldi's compartment and told him he had orders to arrest him. "You must know," said Garibaldi, "that you are committing an illegal action. I am guilty of no crime against the Italian government or its laws. I am a deputy, an Italian general and an American citizen." He reminded Camozzi that he was a general of the Roman Republic too, so at Mentana he had been in his own jurisdiction, had laid down his arms on entering Italy, and if the carabinieri wanted to arrest him they would have to use force. Poor Camozzi sent a telegram to the minister of the interior. "Arrest him," said the reply. Canzio, Crispi and others who were in the carriage seized their arms, the carabinieri fixed bayonets, but Garibaldi thought better of it. Still, in order to show that he yielded only to force, he refused to move, thus forcing the carabinieri to carry him out of the railway coach holding his hands and feet while he remained rigidly motionless like a recalcitrant spoilt child. His behaviour only enhanced his legend.

He was taken to Varignano again, his admirers cheering him at every station. At Varignano he had a nice rest, then Victor Emmanuel graciously allowed him to return to Caprera. With that ended his last armed performance on Italian soil.

IV

The Empress Eugénie once said she would prefer to see the Prussians in Paris to the Italians in Rome. The year 1870 produced both. After Sedan, Garibaldi offered his sword to France, now innocent of his hated enemy, Napoleon III. The first reaction to his offer was not favourable, and it was said even in Italy that the old man simply could not remain quiet in his island home.

"Ah! Mon Dieu il arrive, il ne nous manquait plus que ça," was Crémieux's remark when he heard that Garibaldi was coming to the aid of the French Republic.

"Never," said Gambetta, "would I put a French general under Garibaldi's orders."

At Marseilles Garibaldi was received enthusiastically: not so at Tours. But in France he was, and he made an appearance with Gambetta on the balcony of the mairie of Tours. Then he was given command of all the volunteer forces in France, which became the Army of the Vosges and was sent to defend the line between Besançon and Dijon. The Archbishop of Tours observed: "I thought that Divine Providence had heaped the last measure of humiliation on our country, but I am deceived. There has been reserved for it the supreme humiliation of seeing Garibaldi arrive here, giving himself the mission of saving France." And the Bishop of Autun said: "All his presence among us has achieved is to bring down on our French arms the wrath of Heaven." The bishop's palace was pillaged by Garibaldians, whom Garibaldi had billeted there.

The Army of the Vosges was a pretty motley crowd, what with French, Italian, Polish, Spanish, Hungarian, American and even Pontifical Zouaves volunteers. The marching song had a certain pathos:

Nous partons,
ton, ton,
Comme des moutons,
Comme des moutons,
Pour la boucherie
Pour la boucherie!
Nous aimions
Pourtant la vie.

Mais nous partons,
ton, ton,
Pour la boucherie!
On nous massacrera
ra, ra,
Comme des rats.
Ah! que Bismarck rira!

Garibaldi and General Bordone, his chief of staff, considered themselves very tolerant with those of their troops who did not share their convictions. They allowed, for instance, the Mobiles d'Aveyron to go to church, though, of course, only, as Bordone put it, when their religious convictions did not interfere with the far more important duties of a campaigning army.

One of the first things Garibaldi did as commander-in-chief of the Army of the Vosges was to expel the Jesuits from his territory. The reason he gave was that they signalled at night from Mont-Rolland to the Cathedral of Dôle. He ordered them to remove themselves either to Switzerland or to Lyons. In spite of having assured them that they could return after the war, Garibaldi made himself unpopular with those Frenchmen who thought that it was not for an Italian to expel Frenchmen from France even if they were priests.

There was plenty of robbery and pillaging. General Bordone, who had been but a poor chemist in Avignon before the war, "gladdened the heart of his dear wife in Avignon by sending her boxes with perquisites he had made during the campaign", says Bent. He was the man to whom the indomitable commander-in-chief, who fundamentally only wanted to fight, listened to during the whole campaign. An Italian, Frapolli by name, started his own volunteer corps of two battalions at Chambéry, and forbade his troops to wear the red shirt.

Autun, Dôle and Dijon form a scalene triangle. That triangle was assigned to Garibaldi, the objective being to cover and mask the passage of the Army of the Loire, under General Bourbaki, from the Valley of the Loire to the Valley of the Saone. His son Ricciotti distinguished himself in an attack on 18th November at Culmier-le-sec, the Germans leaving 170 prisoners and their standard behind. At Autun there was other fish to fry. The *Daily News* correspondent found the cathedral occupied by 350 francs-tireurs, one of them reading the *Petit Journal* and smoking a pipe on the high altar.

As in Italy so in France Garibaldi believed that all those

who did not share his opinions were traitors. So he arrested
several priests, tried and convicted them of treasonable
communications with the Germans, but suspending the
death sentence made them march with his soldiers handcuffed for four days. He did, however, apologize to the
bishop when his men robbed him even of his watch and
his crozier.

He was instructed to defend Dijon, which was menaced
by the Germans. On 26th November Garibaldi attacked
the Prussians. In spite of his age and crippling arthritis
the voice and the valour were still as of old. "Forward,
figliuoli," the voice called, "use your bayonets, don't fire
one shot." His close followers listened to him, but the
rest ran when the Prussian vanguard appeared. He tried
to stop them, got out of his carriage, sang to them the
Marseillaise, but it was of no avail. Menotti was dragged
off his horse while he was urging them to stand up to the
Prussians.

The French said that Garibaldi did a lot of harm because
while moving his troops they got in the way of the
transport of the Army of the East. (Blame can always be
easily picked up if one comes to succour the near-defeated.)

Garibaldi's next move was to stay in Dijon, which, he
had been ordered, he should defend *inébranlablement*. That,
apparently, was not right either; for on 21st January
Freycinet sent a telegram to Ricciotti accusing them of
doing nothing to assist General Bourbaki. On the 20th the
Prussians had appeared. Garibaldi drove out in a carriage:
he was too much in pain to mount a horse; and he stayed
on the field of battle giving orders while the battle lasted.
On the second day the Prussians retreated. Ricciotti took a
Prussian flag. He found it lying beside the sixth Prussian
standard-bearer killed while carrying it. "The Army of
the Vosges has again, once more, worked well for the

republic," Garibaldi telegraphed his daughter Teresa. That was the Army's last action.

After the war the Commissioners of Parliamentary Inquiry thought differently. "If General Garibaldi had been a French general, we should have been constrained to ask of you that this report, and the proofs which justify it, should be sent by the Assembly to the Minister of War, with a view to ascertaining if General Garibaldi ought not to be brought up before a court martial to answer for his conduct in having abandoned deliberately, and without contest, the positions which he was commissioned to defend, having thereby caused the loss of one of the French armies and brought about a disaster which can only be compared to the disaster of Sedan and Metz."

". . . he was the only general who fought for France who was not conquered," boomed Victor Hugo in the Assembly to which Garibaldi was elected as deputy for Algeria. Uproar followed. They were not discussing so much the late war as the validity of Garibaldi's election to the Assembly as a foreigner. Victor Hugo's words produced unedifying scenes. Six weeks later the Communists of Paris asked Garibaldi, who resigned from the Assembly, to come among them. "Thank you for the honour of my nomination to the command of the National Guard of Paris," he wrote to them, "which I love, and with which I should have been proud, if health permitted, to share the glory and the danger."

He went back to Caprera declaring he would not wrench his birthplace now from France since France had enough trouble of her own.

V

Garibaldi had written novels. One, *The Thousand*, was about the Thousand; but it was another, *The Rule of the*

Monk, which was a truly lamentable book, with nuns torturing their victims and priests doing no better. "It was a fixed idea with Garibaldi to become as a novelist yet again the regenerator of his people," said Mme Schwartz. "Vain was it for his friends and competent literary critics to oppose the publication of this novel." The *Saturday Review* said: "We would fain hope that the stuff we have been describing was not really written by Garibaldi, but that some hoax had been practised upon the translator and publisher. . . . The book is like the first attempt of an enthusiastic and rather clever lad, after listening to a lecture on Rome from Dr Achilli; and the politics are those of innocent young ladies, who believe everybody who differs from them to be a black-hearted traitor. Such simplicity makes the book almost more pitiable than absurd. . . ." That simplicity was as much part and parcel of the man as of the novel, and one thinks of the man too as the *Saturday Review* goes on to say: ". . . but it is not inconsistent with the possession of certain great qualities which in times of disturbance may convert a tenth-rate novelist into a formidable enemy." The point, however, is that he was a formidable enemy long before he became a tenth-rate novelist.

Tired and disillusioned, Mazzini, the unpardoned exile, died clandestinely, as it were, in Pisa on 10th March 1872. Four days later he was given a public funeral. He died disillusioned because the unification of Italy had not followed the course he had charted for it in his mind. Instead of *l'Italia farà da se* and the Revolution, unification was brought about by the chassepots and bayonets of France, and the distant victories of Prussia. It had been too easy, therefore it could not regenerate the nation. If Victor Emmanuel was the authority, Garibaldi the audacity and Cavour the policy of the Risorgimento, then Mazzini

was the thought. The authority slowly dwindled after
Victor Emmanuel's death, then disappeared; the policy's
logical sequel was the stab in the back of France in 1940,
and Mussolini, who saw himself as the heir of both Mazzini
and Garibaldi, came a cropper, one might say, because in
thought he was Garibaldi and in action Mazzini.

In 1874 Garibaldi was elected deputy of Rome. He went
to Rome. Pio Nono observed: "Lately we were two here;
now we are three." The two were himself, prisoner in the
Vatican, and Victor Emmanuel, king in the Quirinal. But
there was no cause to fear Garibaldi any more. A garrulous
old man, barred by the times and ill-health from the only
sort of action in which he superbly excelled, he was slowly
limping to the grave. He would say: "To the Tarpeian
Rock with the priests, not to the Campidoglio!" He
would offer to the government a policy consisting of three
points: (1) The Nation to be armed; (2) One general tax;
(3) The priests to the mattock. The government would
not pay heed to him. Depretis, who had been his pro-
dictator in Sicily, as prime minister in 1876 gave him a
pension. Shortly after, Garibaldi called him a subservient
lackey of the king.

On 7th January 1878 Victor Emmanuel died and Pio
Nono followed him on 7th February. Garibaldi's turn
came on 2nd June 1882.

"Yesterday," certified two doctors on 3rd June, "at
6 p.m., General Giuseppe Garibaldi died at his home in
Caprera of pharyngeal paralysis."

It was Garibaldi's wish that he should be cremated. His
widow, Menotti, the Canzios, Francesco Crispi, Alberto
Mario and others met to discuss the obsequies. After some
argument it was decided to have his body embalmed and
leave the decision to the Italian parliament. On 8th June,
in the presence of Prince Tommaso, representing King

Umberto, two ministers, the presidents of Senate and Chamber, and representatives of the Navy, the Army, the Thousand and the Volunteers, he was buried contrary to his expressed desire. He lies in Caprera.

"In history," said Mme Schwartz, who lived till 1889, "Garibaldi will always shine resplendent as a sun; but even the sun has its spots."

NOTES ON SOME PERSONS
MENTIONED IN THE BOOK

AGOSTINO BERTANI (1812–1886): A participant in the revolution of 1848, he served as a medical officer and organized the ambulance service for the Roman Republic of 1849. In 1859 he joined Garibaldi's forces as a surgeon and was later appointed secretary-general at Naples where he founded twelve infant asylums and prepared for the suppression of the religious orders. Elected to parliament in 1861 he opposed Garibaldi's expedition which ended at Aspromonte but continued to treat Garibaldi in his medical capacity. In 1866 he organized the medical service for Garibaldi's troops and in the following year took an active part in the fighting at Mentana. In parliament he was leader of the extreme left and as a deputy was particularly active in promoting a public health system.

LOUIS BLANC (1811–1882): French politician and historian born in Madrid where his father was Joseph Bonaparte's inspector-general of finance. He founded in Paris the *Revue du progrès*. In 1841 he published his *Histoire de dix ans* attacking Louis Philippe. In 1848 he joined the provisional government, later was forced to fly to England where he remained till 1871, then returned to France. His political and social ideas had a deep influence on Socialism in France.

ENRICO COSENZ (1812–1898): He served in the Neapolitan artillery against the Austrians in 1848, and took part in the defence of Venice; in 1859 became commander of a Garibaldian regiment; in 1860 he led the Garibaldian expedition to Sicily, defeating two Neapolitan brigades at Piale. In Naples he was appointed minister of war and helped to organize the plebiscite. From 1881 till his death he held the post of chief of the general staff.

FRANCESCO CRISPI (1819–1901): A Sicilian, born at Ribera, Crispi established himself as a lawyer in Naples in 1846 until 1848 when he took an active part in the revolution. With the restoration of the Bourbons he was compelled to flee and until 1859 was in exile in Malta, Paris and London where he joined forces with Mazzini. In 1859 he returned to Italy and helped to organize the expedition of the Thousand. He later served in the Sicilian provisional government. Elected as a deputy in 1861 he was an aggressive republican but in 1864 he switched his support to the monarchy which he considered to be the only means of uniting Italy. In 1876 he became president of the chamber of deputies and in 1877 became minister of the interior. The accession of Umberto I enabled Crispi to secure the formal establishment of the monarchy as ruler over the whole of Italy. He was also instrumental in persuading the sacred college to hold the conclave in Rome which elected Leo XIII as Pope. Compelled to resign office on a charge of bigamy he returned briefly to office as minister of the interior in 1887.

LAJOS (LOUIS) KOSSUTH (1802-1894): Hungarian politician, journalist, orator, leader of the Hungarian revolution of 1848, Dictator of Hungary 1849, escaped after defeat of revolution to Turkey, came to England in 1851, moved on to America, returned to England where he lived for eight years in close connection with Mazzini. In 1859 entered into negotiations with Napoleon III. The negotiations were brought to naught by the Peace of Villafranca. He remained in Italy, and died in Turin; his body was taken to Budapest where he was buried amid the mourning of the whole nation. Holyoake considered him one of the finest orators in the English language of his time.

GIUSEPPE LA FARINA (1815-1863): A Sicilian author and politician, he was born at Messina and in 1837 went into exile after taking part in an insurrection. Two years later he returned to Sicily and directed several Liberal newspapers before returning to exile in Florence. Again in Sicily in 1848, he fled to France, returning six years later to Italy where he settled at Turin. During 1856 he founded the *Piccolo Corriere d'Italia* and played a leading role in Cavour's policy by advocating the unification of Italy under Victor Emmanuel, organizing the recruitment of volunteers from all over Italy for the Piedmontese army and supporting Garibaldi's expedition to Sicily. He also acted as an intermediary between Cavour and Garibaldi. In 1860 he was chosen as a member of the first Italian parliament and later became a councillor of state.

CHRISTOPHE LÉON LOUIS JUCHAULT DE LA MORICIÈRE (1806-1865): Born at Nantes, he was one of Bugeaud's most efficient and distinguished generals in Algeria of which he was for a time acting governor-general. In 1848, the year following his capture of Abd el-Kader, he was elected to the Chamber of Deputies and later served as minister of war. A leading opponent of Louis Napoleon, he was arrested and exiled after the latter's *coup d'état* in 1852. In 1860 he accepted the command of the papal forces and in April of that year was defeated by the Italian army at Castelfidardo. Five years later he died in France where he had been allowed to return.

ALEXANDRE AUGUSTE LEDRU-ROLLIN (1807-1874): French lawyer and politician. His opposition to the policy of Louis Napoleon, especially his

Roman policy, led to his moving the impeachment of the president and his ministers. On his escape to London he joined the revolutionary committee of Europe with Kossuth and Mazzini. He returned to France after twenty years of exile. In 1871 though elected he refused to sit in the National Assembly. In 1874, the year of his death, he became member for Vaucluse. He made large contributions to French jurisprudence.

GOFFREDO MAMELI (1827–1849): Italian poet and patriot. He wrote a hymn to the Bandiera brothers, also *Fratelli d'Italia* (now the Italian national anthem), and was devoted to Mazzini. He was wounded on April 30, 1849, during the defence of Rome, but resumed his place in the ranks on June 3, was wounded again and died of his wounds on July 6.

DANIELE MANIN (1804–1857): Born at Venice, the son of a Jewish convert to Catholicism, Manin studied law at Padua and later practised in his native city until he was arrested in 1848. Popular agitation forced the Austrian governor to release him and he later became president of the Venetian republic until he resigned his powers to the Piedmontese commissioners. In 1849 he was again elected president to organize resistance to the Austrians after the defeat of Novara. After the collapse of the republic Manin went into exile in Paris where he became a leader of the Italian expatriates, founding with Pallavicini and La Farina the Società Nazionale Italiana. Eleven years after his death his remains were taken to Venice and he was honoured with a public funeral.

FELICE ORSINI (1819–1858): Italian revolutionary. Implicated with his father in revolutionary plots, he was arrested in 1844, and condemned to imprisonment for life. Pio Nono released him. He was a member of the Roman Constituent assembly in 1849. He was arrested in 1854 in Mantua, but escaped a few months later. His book *Austrian Dungeons in Italy* led to a rupture between him and Mazzini. On January 14, 1858, he and his accomplices threw three bombs at the French Emperor and Empress who were on their way to the theatre. He was arrested and from prison wrote a letter to the Emperor exhorting him to take up the cause of Italy. He was executed on March 13.

URBANO RATTAZZI (1808–1873): Born at Alessandria, Rattazzi practised at the bar until 1848 when he was sent to the chamber of deputies in Turin to represent his native town. After holding various offices, the defeat of Novara compelled him to resign. In 1852 he was elected president of the chamber, resigning in 1858. After a period of office as minister of the interior in 1859–60 he was entrusted with the formation of a new ministry in 1862 but his policy of repression towards Garibaldi at Aspromonte led to his fall later that year. He was prime minister again in 1867 and died at Frosinone six years later.

BETTINO RICASOLI (1809–1880): Known as the "Iron Baron", he was born at Broglio. In 1847 he founded the journal *La Patria* and in 1859 as Tuscan minister of the interior he promoted the union of Tuscany with Piedmont. In 1861 he became a deputy and later succeeded Cavour as Premier. He was responsible for admitting Garibaldi's volunteers to the regular army and revoking the decree of exile against Mazzini. After resigning in 1862 he returned to power in 1866 when he refused Napoleon III's offer to cede Venetia to Italy and attempted to conciliate the Vatican by offering to restore the Church's property. The Vatican accepted Ricasoli's proposals but the chamber of deputies refused and was dissolved. Ricasoli resigned office.

BIBLIOGRAPHY

ABBA, G. C., *Da Quarto al Volturno. Noterelle d'uno dei Mille*, Ed. 5.

BANDI, GIUSEPPE, *Anita Garibaldi, con documenti sulla vita di Garibaldi in America*, R. Bemporad & F. Editori, Firenze, 1932.

I Mille, 1906 edn.

BARRILI, A. G., *Con Garibaldi alle porte di Roma*, 1867.

BENT, J. T., *Life of Garibaldi*, 1881.

BERKELEY, G. F.-H., *The Irish Battalion in the Papal Army of 1860*, The Talbot Press Limited, Dublin & Cork, 1929.

BERKELEY, G. F.-H. & MRS., *Italy in the Making: 1815–1846*, 1909.

BIANCHI, NICOMEDE, *Il Conte Camillo Cavour. Documenti editi e inediti*, Torino, 1863.

BORDONE, GENERAL, *Garibaldi et l'Armée des Vosges*, Librairie Internationale, Paris, 1871.

CASTELLINI, G., *Pagine Garibaldine 1848–66*, 1909.

CHAMBER, O. W. S., *Garibaldi and Italian Unity*, 1864.

COLET, LOUISE, *L'Italie des Italiens*.

CURATULO, G. E., *Garibaldi e le donne*, Imprimerie Polyglotte, Roma, 1913.

Garibaldi, Vittorio Emmanuele, Cavour nei fasti della patria. Documenti inediti, 1911.

Il dissidio tra Mazzini e Garibaldi. Documenti inediti, 1928.

DESCUDIER, A., *Mémoires authentiques sur Garibaldi: les évènements de Sicile*, 1864.

DICEY, EDWARD, *Cavour: A Memoir*, Cambridge, Macmillan, London, 1861.

DUMAS, ALEXANDRE, *The Memoirs of Garibaldi*; translated by R. S. Garnett, with contributions by George Sand and Victor Hugo; Ernest Benn, London, 1931.

FRATELLINI, SALVATORE, *Spoleto nel Risorgimento Nazionale*; Publicazione per il Cinquantennario della liberazione di Spoleto, 17 settembre 1910.

FRISCHAUER: *Garibaldi, the Man and the Nation,* 1935.

GAIANI, E., *Garibaldi ed i cacciatori delle Alpi 1859–1909.*

GARIBALDI, GIUSEPPE, *The Rule of the Monk* (2 vols.), Cassell, Petter & Galpin, London.

I Mille, 1874.

Memorie.

GUERZONI, GIUSEPPE, *Garibaldi,* Firenze, G. Bàrbera, 1882.

HALES, E. E. Y., *Pio Nono,* Eyre & Spottiswoode, London, 1954.

HAYWARD, FERNAND, *Pie IX et son temps,* Plon, Paris, 1948.

HOLYOAKE, GEORGE JACOB, *Bygones Worth Remembering.* *Sixty Years of an Agitator's Life,* T. Fisher Unwin, London.

IDEVILLE, COMTE HENRI D', *Journal d'un Diplomate en Italie,* I. Turin 1859–62; 2. Rome 1862–6.

Illustrated Life and Career of Garibaldi, Ward & Lock, London.

KING, BOLTON, *A History of Italian Unity, 1814–1871,* 1898; 2 vols.

Mazzini, Dent, 1902.

LARG, DAVID, *Giuseppe Garibaldi: A Biography,* Peter Davies, London, 1934.

LEYNADIER, CAMILLE, *Mémoires authentiques sur Garibaldi,* Arthème Fayard—Arnaud de Vresse Libraires, Paris, 1864.

LOEVINSON, H. E., *Giuseppe Garibaldi e la sua legione nello stato romano 1848–9,* 1902–7.

MACK-SMITH, D., *Garibaldi,* Hutchinson, 1957.

MARIO, A., *Garibaldi,* 1879.

The Red Shirt, Episodes, 1865.

MARIO, J. W., Posthumous Papers of Jessie Wright Mario edited, with introduction notes and epilogue, by the Duke Litta-Visconti-Arese: *The Birth of Modern Italy,* T. Fisher Unwin, London, 1909.

MARIO, M., *L'onesto di Garibaldi,* 1913.

MARRIOTT, J. A. R., *Makers of Modern Italy,* 1931.

McGRIGOR, Sir C. R., *Garibaldi at Home,* 1866.

MELENA, ELPIS [Marie E. von Schwartz]: *Recollections of Garibaldi. Recollections of his Life, with Letters,* 1887. (English translations of *Denkwürdigkeiten. Garibaldi's Denkwürdigkeiten,* 1861.)

MIDDLETON, ROBERT, *Garibaldi, ses opérations en l'armée des Vosges*, Garnier frères, Paris, 1872.

MUNDY, REAR-ADMIRAL SIR RODNEY, K.C.B., *H.M.S. "Hannibal" at Palermo and Naples during the Italian Revolution*, John Murray, London, 1863.

NAZARI-MICHELI, I., *Cavour e Garibaldi nel 1860*, 1911.

PUCCIONI, N., *Garibaldi nei canti dei poeti*, 1912.

RASCH, G. H., *Garibaldi e Napoli nel 1860*, 1938.

ROMUSSI, C., *Garibaldi nelle medaglie*, 1905.

SFORZA, G., *Garibaldi in Toscana nel 1848*, 1897.

STIAVELLI, G., *Garibaldi nella letteratura italiana*, 1907.

The Seven Hills Magazine, edited by The Oliver Plunket Society, Rome; James Duffy & Co. Limited, March, 1908.

TREVELYAN, GEORGE MACAULAY, *Garibaldi and the Making of Italy. June–November, 1860*, Longmans, London, 1911.

Garibaldi and the Thousand, May, 1860, Longmans, London, 1909.

Garibaldi's Defence of the Roman Republic, 1848–9, Longmans, London, 1907.

VECCHI, COLONEL, *Garibaldi at Caprera*, translated from the Italian, with preface by Mrs Gaskell, Macmillan, London, 1862.

WINNINGTON, INGRAM, *Hearts of Oak*, 1889.

INDEX

(G. = Giuseppe Garibaldi. References to a continuous series of pages, e.g. 87–94, do not necessarily indicate continuous treatment.)